Pioneer Theatre in the Boise Basin
1863-1899

Pioneer Theatre in the Boise Basin
1863-1899

by

Charles E. Lauterbach, Ph.D.
Professor Emeritus, Theatre Arts
Boise State University

CreateSpace

Copyright©, 2013

by

CHARLES E. LAUTERBACH

LIBRARY OF CONGRESS CONTROL NUMBER: 2012955775

ISBN 978-0-615-73445-3

Cover Design: Kristi Simmons and Amber Hawton-Hill

Marketing by Design

D edicated to my mother and father, Emma and Carl, for providing the means for my education and to my wife Margaret who has encouraged and supported my endeavors through these many years.

Table of Contents

Illustrations

(Continued)

Illustrations

Acknowledgements

Jim and Stella Schneider have given valuable personal encouragement during the creation of this work and Jim's advice on publishing and his aid with computer and software concerns has been invaluable.

Margaret Lauterbach, in addition to helping guide research, has also served as a copy editor and constructive critic.

Judith Austin has contributed to applications for grants and supplied budgetary information.

The entire staff of the Boise City Department of Arts and History created the opportunity to bring this study to the public and have contributed a great deal of time and effort to see it completed.

While grants from Boise State University, the State Board of Education and the Idaho Humanities Council were not involved directly in the publication of this study, they did aid in the author's research about theatre in the western United States in the nineteenth and early twentieth century.

The staffs of special collections in the libraries of the following universities or historical societies have made possible the many photographs in this book. Thanks to Nicolette Bromberg from the Special Collections department of the University of Washington for arranging production rights for most of the photographs in this book. Thomas Lisante helped obtain rights to nine pictures from The New York Public Library's famed Billy Rose Theatre Collection. Others who contributed were Krissy Giacoletto with the Special

Collections division of the J. Willard Marriott Library at the University of Utah, Jenaleigh Kiebert and David Matte of the Idaho State Historical Society and Gregory M. Walz of the Utah Historical Society. Other pictures were supplied by the University of Nevada, the Meserve Collection of the Houghton Library at Harvard University and the University of Victoria (Australia).

Pioneers! Oh, Pioneers!

[Excepts from a poem by Walt Whitman]

O you youths, Western youths,
So impatient, full of action, full of manly pride and friendship,
Plain I see you, Western youths, see you tramping with the foremost,
Pioneers! O Pioneers!

We detachments steady throwing
Down the edges, through the passes, up the mountain steep,
Conquering, holding, daring, venturing as we go the unknown ways,
Pioneers! O Pioneers!

We primeval forests felling,
We the rivers stemming, vexing we and piercing deep the mines within,
We the surface broad surveying, we the virgin soil upheaving,
Pioneer! O Pioneers!

Colorado men are we,
From the peaks gigantic, from the great sierras and the high plateaus,
From the mine and from the gully, from the hunting trail we come,
Pioneers! O Pioneers!

Introduction

In the last three decades of the nineteenth century American communities took civic pride in being labeled "show towns," a term denoting a city as supportive of a large number and variety of theatrical entertainments. Show towns shared three elements. First there had to be a connection to the national railroad system that carried hundreds of plays, musicals and other forms of theatrical entertainment across the nation. Second, a town needed theatre venues with stages large enough to accommodate the scenic demands of often elaborate productions and auditoriums capable of seating enough patrons to assure at least some box office profit for both producers and local theatre managers. Lastly, there had to be a population large enough and wealthy enough to attend the theatres on a frequent and reliable basis.

This book is a historical narrative describing in a chronological form how Boise City, a remote mining supply town in the Idaho territory, overcame several obstacles between 1863 and 1900 to become a "show town." These obstacles included a lack of a connection to the national railroad system, inadequate theatre facilities and too small a population to attract and support anything more than small, usually regional theatre companies.

This history is important because to date no complete history of early theatrical entertainments in the Boise Basin has been written. In effect, it is a rare history of theatre in Boise and surrounding mining towns during both the territorial and state eras. It documents the steps by which the citizens of a small, remote community established the basis of support for what is today; a vital and diverse theatrical scene in one of the largest metropolitan areas in the Pacific Northwest. Finally, it adds another book to the relatively small collection of books about the nineteenth century theatre in the American West.

Except for a master's thesis by Robert F. Eggers (*A History of Theatre in Boise, Idaho from 1863 to 1963*. Unpublished M.A. Thesis, University of Oregon, 1963), no comprehensive study has been made of theatrical activity in Idaho's capital city. The main strength of Egger's thesis is an extensive play list of shows performed in Boise by date, place and producing company. This list has been replicated for this study and several omissions and wrong dates were detected. Egger's text for his thesis is less than one-hundred pages long and covers 100 years. While it furnishes a broad outline of theatre in Boise, it fails to adequately cover the nuances of Boise theatre productions.

In addition to Egger's thesis, other authors have dealt in part with early entertainments in the Boise Basin. Fred Gilliards' "Early Theatre in the Owyhees" and his "Pioneer Dramatists in the Boise Basin" examine early theatre in Silver City, Idaho and Idaho City, Idaho. However, his articles mainly present a simple statistical analysis of the types and forms of dramas presented in the mining towns and only incidentally include historical concerns. The author of this book wrote two articles about early theatre in Idaho City which appeared in the *Idaho Magazine* in 2007. [See, Bibliography.]

A few books about the general history of Boise and the Boise Basin contain mentions of early theatrical entertainments. Annie Laurie Bird's *Boise: The Peace Valley* has a six page section on entertainments, but focuses more on libraries, lodges, dog fights and raffles than on theatre, devoting just two sentences on the subject. Arthur A. Hart's informative book, *Basin of Gold: Life in the Boise Basin:1862-1890,* contains just three entertaining pages about popular Irish violinist, John Kelly, but has little else about theatre entertainment. Merle Well's well known, *Boise: An Illustrated History*, has very little about theatricals except for a few pictures of Boise amateur productions with brief comments in the picture captions. The latest Boise history, Carol MacGregor's *Boise, Idaho, 1882-1910: Prosperity in Isolation,* contains a three page general commentary on the arts in Boise between 1881 and 1910, but, except for few anecdotes, does not deal with theatre at any length. While the above sources have little to do with theatrical entertainments, readers who would like to know more about the political, social, economic and other conditions of the time are urged to consult them. [Note: full citations for the above sources are listed in the "Bibliography" section at the end of this book.]

While three-quarters of this narrative focuses on the development of theatre entertainments in Boise City, the initial chapter includes an extensive treatment of theatre activity in the Boise Basin mining towns of Idaho City and Silver City. This not only enriches the story of early entertainments, but supplies a regional context for the events occurring in what would become the capital city of Idaho. After the mining boom in the Boise Basin largely subsided after 1870, a few small troupes that played in Boise occasionally took side trips to perform in Idaho City and Silver City up to the 1880's. These appearances are not documented mainly due to lack of sources and to avoid repetitive detail. But it was Boise that maintained a continuity of theatrical events to the end of the century. Although this history is organized by decades, there is one exception. The material on Silver City between 1870 and 1876 is included in the 1860 chapter in order to complete the record of theatrical activity in that area in a continuous and cohesive manner.

The term "theatrical entertainments," which often appears in this study, is used to encompass a wide range of performance activity and not just the performance of a literary work by a group of actors. It includes most forms of diversion involving a performer or performers for an audience: dramas, comedies, melodramas, farces, operas, circuses, minstrel shows, medicine shows, "elocutionists," equestrian shows, magicians, mind readers, hypnotists, dog and pony shows, variety shows (vaudeville) and even various musical events. Other forms of entertainment such a sports, social dances and gambling are beyond the scope of the present study.

Although many play titles are included in the following pages, the plays themselves are described only briefly or not at all. The latter half of the nineteenth century saw few American plays of lasting merit. They were intended to be entertainment vehicles for an immediate audience much like the television situation comedies of today. For this reason the reader will not be burdened with the recapitulation of formulaic plots, the description of obviously stock characters the citation of usually trite dialogue nor a statement of shopworn themes.

This book is as complete a record of theatrical entertainments in the Boise and the Boise Basin as the author's research was able to uncover and may contain more detail than a casual reader may be interested in. If so inclined, readers may want to skip over some listings of plays and players to get to the many colorful anecdotes, events and biographic commentary.

In order to give a suggestion of the spirit and tone of the nineteenth century in Idaho, quotes from the then contemporary newspapers are included in abundance. Other sources are cited to provide brief biographic comments on some of the major figures or performers of the period.

Lastly, the reader is invited to enjoy the trials and tribulations of pioneer Boise inhabitants as they established and nurtured theatrical entertainments in spite of long odds against them. Their efforts eventually resulted in the vigorous and diverse theatre presentations available to Boise's citizens at the present time.

CHAPTER 1

Gold Rush Theatre

Idaho City, Silver City and Boise, Idaho
1863-1869

Prologue

Southwest Idaho's entertainment history began in the 1860's with various theatrical events in two pioneer gold mining communities, Idaho City and Silver City, and a major mining supply station, Boise City. These and smaller towns such as Placerville, Centerville and Pioneer constituted the geographic location that came to be known as the Boise Basin. Gold strikes in the Basin attracted thousands of fortune hunters that within one year swelled the population for the area to over fifteen thousand. Idaho City alone surpassed Portland, Oregon in number of inhabitants. Gold fever and an exploding population provided the setting for the first significant professional and amateur "theatricals" in the territory that would become the state of Idaho.

Gold prospecting brought men into what is now northern Idaho as early as 1860. Following some strikes in that area, prospectors and miners dropped southward into the Boise basin in search of new bonanzas. On August 2, 1862 a group called the Grimes party found gold at a stream in an area called Boston Bar, near a location that later became the town of Centerville. Word of the strike reached gold seekers in the Pacific Northwest who quickly immigrated into the territory in huge numbers. Within two months they had established the towns of Hog'em and Bannock City, located some forty miles north of what is now Boise, Idaho. Bannock City, also called West Bannock, became known as Idaho City and there the annals of the Boise Basin's theatrical history began.

By October of 1863, within fourteen months of the August 2, 1862 discovery of gold on Boston Bar, a newspaper in Idaho City reported nightly variety entertainments at a local saloon. In the next three years the city's residents experienced a theatrical production boom and, along with the citizens of nearby mining towns, attended plays by several professional companies. By 1867 many miners had left in search of new bonanzas and the curtain closed on Idaho's first theatrical ventures.

No sooner had the curtain rung down in Idaho City when theatre surfaced in Silver City and surrounding Owyhee mountain towns. Here, some thirty miles south west of Boise City, professional and amateur groups provided amusements until 1874 when this community, too, experienced the migration of miners to more promising claims.

Boise City, although not a mining camp, had its role to play in the history of Idaho pioneer theatre. Various touring troupes seeking their fortunes in the mining camps had to pass through the town on their way to either of the two mining areas and took advantage of the situation by playing brief local engagements. During the winter months miners sought a relatively milder climate at lower elevations which added significantly to the population, a condition attractive to enterprising theatrical managers.

Idaho City
1863

The earliest record of entertainment in Idaho City appeared in the October 13, 1863 edition of the *Boise News*. An ad announced "Kelly's Varieties at Washoe Saloon" nightly at 8:00 p.m. and listed singing, and dancing by an "unrivaled troupe of performers" as chief attractions. Admission ranged from fifty cents for parquet to one dollar for the orchestra section and front seats, locations "reserved for the ladies."[1]

Kelly's Varieties, also called "Minstrels," played at the Washoe Saloon as well as Kelly and Marshall's Theatre through at least December 5, 1863. Performers mentioned in the press of the time were John and Willie Kelly, Virginia Maning, Moulton and Tommy Briggs.[2]

John Kelly, one of the best known performers in the Pacific Northwest and Montana territories, possessed exceptional skill as a violinist, capable of creating a range of music that could either wet the eyes of an audience with sentimental ballads or set toes to tapping with joyful dance tunes. Kelly displayed additional talents for singing, doing character sketches (then called "delineations") and acting in short farces.

Under Kelly's tutelage Willie Kelly, a Shoshoni boy who had been adopted by Kelly after the child's parents had been murdered by a white raiding party, learned to play the violin and mastered several clever feats of contortion and acrobatics. Both Kellys continued to perform in various towns of the Idaho territory throughout the 1860's. Moulton, noted as a comic singer , too, appeared frequently in conjunction with Idaho minstrel and theatric endeavors of the period.[3]

Despite the winter weather, theatre activity increased in December of 1863 with the opening of two theatres. By December 12, J. J. Allison opened the Idaho Theatre that featured "historical and musical entertainments" with Mrs. Mitchell and a magic company headed by Professor Myers.[4] Around Christmas Professor Myers had fitted up his own theatre, named The Magic Temple, which he advertised as having a private entrance for ladies "exclusive from the Saloon portion of the building."[5]

The Idaho Theatre had a rather short existence. Allison performed there through January 9 of 1864 and then toured to nearby Placerville and Centerville as the theatre underwent remodeling and refitting. Upon his return he played a personal benefit and during the first week of February produced a new local play, *A Hit at the Time*, a work filled with allusions to local history. By February 20 the Idaho Theatre ceased to exist. On that day the paper printed that the building once occupied by the Idaho Theatre was fast assuming the shape of a courthouse with witness stands, jury boxes and the like.[6]

Professor Myers fared better at The Magic Temple where he, Mrs. Mitchell, Mrs. Van Houton, J.B. Smith, Mrs. Overbeck and, sometimes, the McGinley family attracted sufficient patronage to stay in business. Their repertory consisted of old popular standards such as *Don Cesar De Bazan* and *The Harp of Altenburg*, a play that Myers, when faced with a scarcity of playbooks, allegedly recreated from memory after a lapse of twenty-five years.[7]

Even as Professor Myers' Company continued its success, competitors drafted plans for a rival theatre, The Forrest, named after America's first famous native born actor, Edwin Forrest, opened on Feb. 20, 1864 with a program of *Pleasant Neighbor* or *The Merry Cobbler* and during the first week productions of *Two Gregories* and *Two Bonifaces* played there. In its second week George Brower directed and starred in *The Harlequin's Revenge* which "considering the want of facilities for rigging stage machinery, was admirably played."[8] Shortly after this the management added a new painted backdrop representing a city street with lampposts and houses. The spacious Forrest Theatre featured a drop curtain representing the Hellespont and Leander's tower "with Leander standing in front contemplating the cottage, or its inmate, on the opposite shore."[9]

The news of the engagement of H.B. Lane as manager of the Forrest Theatre appeared in the April 10 paper. Along with a Mr. Chapman, Lane set about to acquire a company of first-class San Francisco talent. Before "going below" to California, Mr. Lane entertained Forrest Theatre patrons with his own program of Shakespearean readings and on April 10 and 16 appeared in the title role of *The Toodles* supported by Mrs. Pernicia Sheppard and a well known member of the Idaho bar, I. N. Smith. On April 18 the same company presented a nineteenth century favorite, *The Lady of Lyons*, for the first time in Idaho City.[10]

Competition from the Forrest Theatre enterprise provoked changes in its rival theatre. An announcement of plans for enlarging The Magic Temple (also called Magic Palace and Temple Theatre) appeared in the press on March 19, 1864. Remodeling, under the supervision of Professor Myers and a Mr. Hamilton, increased the seating to 800 in a building measuring 102 feet deep with a stage twenty-seven feet deep and thirty-seven feet wide. The beautifully decorated theatre contained "four private boxes, dress circle, orchestra, parquet, gallery, and all the usual appurtenances of a first-class San Francisco theatre."[11] The all-but-new playhouse, renamed The Jenny Lind Theatre in honor of the famous Swedish Nightingale, opened on April 23 with a performance of *La Borita* featuring the Peterson brothers.[12]

Up to May of 1864 Idaho City theatricals had been presented by troupes composed of a few local professionals augmented by amateurs from the town. The arrival of the Leighton company from its engagement in Walla Walla on April 30 signaled the beginning of truly professional theatre in the Idaho territory. Mrs. W. H. Leighton, billed as the "Queen of Comedy and Song,"[13] led the company that also included Miss Belle Douglas, A. R. Phelps, J. E. Myers, B. S. Mortimer, Mr. and Mrs. Leslie, John S. Potter, J. Townsend, W. H. Hamilton and E. Myers.[14]

John S. Potter, the most important of this group of performers, had earned a national reputation in his art. Pursuit of his career as actor and manager, which began in the 1840's, had taken him literally from coast to coast. Earlier in his career he had appeared in cities as separated as Richmond, Virginia and Rochester, New York. Just before he came to Idaho, he had spent some time in Portland,

Oregon. Sol Smith, himself a noted theatre manager, remarked that Potter had opened (and closed) more theatres than any other manager in American theatre.[15]

Mrs. W.H. Leighton, after a successful season at Laura Keene's theatre in New York, journeyed to California in the fall of 1861 and became a decided hit there with her good looks, grace and singing ability. Following her success in California, she toured through the interior of the Nevada territory with appearances in

Mrs. W. H. Leighton
Picture History
MES13614

Carson City in September of 1862.[16] After returning to California she continued to tour in that state, made some return appearances in Nevada and played in various Pacific Northwest towns before eventually arriving in the Idaho region. By 1865 she had returned to New York to perform at the New Bowery Theatre.

After arriving in Idaho City the Leighton company spent a week preparing for its engagement by rehearsing a repertoire of plays, arranging for appropriate scenery and drumming up publicity for the season. On May 7 the players opened at the Jenny Lind Theatre with J. G. Rosenbaum listed as proprietor and A. R. Phelps as manager. Private box admissions sold for up to sixteen dollars, dress circle cost two dollars and even the "pit" went for a dollar.[17]

High prices for tickets prevailed in the professional theatre era of mining camps that suffered chronically from generally inflated costs. Early prospectors, who did not work for wages, paid for admission in gold they had panned or mined. Later the miners who worked for others only earned two to three dollars for a long day of physically taxing labor. They paid admission to a theatre that equaled one-third or more of that amount. No doubt theatre managers and performers saw mining boom towns as places offering opportunities for earning great profits. On the other hand the theatre managers assumed tremendous expenses in the form of actor's salaries, transportation to remote localities, theatre rentals, settings, royalties, etc. While the seemingly admission prices may seem exhorbitant, the cost was well suited the economic conditions.

At the same time the Leighton company began its engagement at the Jenny Lind Theatre a local variety group titled the Cosmopolitan Theatrical Troupe left to tour various camps throughout the basin. Scheduled to perform at Kimball's Saloon in Placerville on May 7, the troupe included several "veterans" of the local entertainment scene. Its ranks included George Brower, a versatile actor; Sheppard, a jig dancer; Moulton, a comic singer; Holman, a banjoist; Mr. Chapman, a violinist; Mrs. Sheppard, a young and pleasing beginner; and Mrs. Baker, a charming vocalist.[18] Judging from the talents listed for the performers, the company, in spite of its title, probably specialized more in variety entertainment than in theatrical productions.

The Leighton company drew crowded houses throughout May and early June at the Jenny Lind. Their performances of such familiar works as *The Stranger*, *Uncle Tom's Cabin* and *The Octoroon* often earned extravagant praise for Mrs. Leighton in the leading roles. While she played serious roles effectively, comic roles best fitted her talents. The local press regarded her as the funniest woman alive with "comicalities . . . as funny to her as to any of the audience."[19] Often her exuberant spirit led her to find a funny spot even in the most solemn scene—especially if her eye happened to catch that of some equally appreciative "cuss" in the audience. This "queen of comedy and song" played several engagements with other companies before leaving town on July 26, 1864.

In late May of 1864 the Idaho City theatrical scene grew more competitive with the arrival of two new theatrical troupes. On May 28 the Robinson company arrived for an engagement at the Forrest Theatre and on May 29 the George Waldron troupe occupied the Jenny Lind theatre, vacated only the day before by the Leighton players.

The Robinson Family Company, when first noted in the mining camp paper, consisted of manager John Robinson; his daughter, Sue Robinson Getzler; his son, William; his wife, Clara; his son-in-law, Charles Getzler plus H. B. Lane, Mr. and Mrs. Sheppard, Mr. Manly and Mr. Smith.[20] The Robinsons began their theatrical enterprise in the San Francisco area during the California gold rush and had traveled extensively in the Pacific Northwest.[21]

Sue Robinson Getzler, the "particular bright star" of the Robinson family opened her career as a child star of considerable talent and charm. Through experience and training she developed into a versatile entertainer who could act, sing and dance with equal and laudable effectiveness. During her 1864 stay in Idaho City she played lead or major roles in such noted dramas as *The Lady of Lyons*, *Black-Eyed Susan*, *Ingomar* and *Camille*. Between acts she frequently entertained by dancing or singing sentimental ballads. She had married Charles Getzler in Walla Walla, Washington shortly before departing for the Idaho territory. During her Idaho City engagement, she announced, with many a protest from spectator and newspaper editor, her plans to retire from the stage. In spite of her intentions, she returned to play Idaho towns in both 1865 and 1866. According to conflicting sources she died at Sacramento either sometime in 1867 or in July of 1871.[22]

George Waldron, too, had earned a solid reputation with theatre patrons in the Pacific Northwest, particularly those of San Francisco and Portland where he proved a popular actor and manager. After initial experiences as a shoemaker and a sailor, he became stage struck in San Francisco in 1854 and quickly established a career as a leading man.[23] His company, made up of "imported" talent augmented by local professionals, consisted of Mrs. Waldron, E. Reeves, Robert H. Lindsay, J. E. Myers, Miss Minnie Gillispie, H .B. Lane and Mr. Hamilton.[24] From May 29 to June 5 Waldron and his company presented *Othello*, *Prisoner of Doom*, *Marble Heart*, *La Tour de Nesle* and *Nick of the Woods*. This fare did not attract the patronage it warranted, meeting with but indifferent success, for as the *Boise*

George Waldron
Utah State Historical Society
PC9790

News observed: "The public mind is evidently not in a mood for heavy tragedy."[25] After this failure Waldron's company broke up. Most members joined a touring troupe put together by Henry and McGinley, but Waldron united forces with the John S. Potter Company at the Forrest Theatre.

By mid-June of 1864, John Potter and John Robinson had merged their companies and added some new performers, notably George Pardey, a comedian from Colorado, and Mrs. Leighton who had remained in town after her company disbanded. This realignment of performers and reorganization of companies occurred with some regularity during the course of theatre operations in Idaho City with the result that some performers' names shifted about in newspaper reviews and other theatrical items in a most confusing manner.

Through June and July the Potter, Robinson and Waldron combination performed three or more times a week at the Forrest Theatre, with only occasional appearances at the Jenny Lind, in such old favorites as *Lucretia Borgia*, *Rob Roy* and *Camille* as well as the Shakespearean plays of *Hamlet* and *Richard III*. Waldron played the dramatic leads and the versatile Sue Getzler acted major female roles in both comedies and tragedies.

When Charles Getzler's lease on the Forrest Theatre expired on August 6, Robinson and Potter ended their management partnership and Robinson took his family on a tour to Placerville and other sites in the Basin. They returned to Idaho City by August 20 to give a final series of benefit performances before leaving the territory at which time Sue Getzler once more declared her intentions to leave the profession. About this same time Potter and Waldron journeyed to Boise to play a short season there. They returned by August 26 to meet with their new leading lady, the famous, nationally renowned tragedienne, Mrs. Julia Dean Hayne. In order to get to Idaho City she had endured a "perilous journey by sea and land" including "a three days storm on the steamer Pacific in coming up from San Francisco."[26] Despite the rigors of travel, Mrs. Hayne immediately entered into rehearsals with Potter's troupe and opened three days later at the Jenny Lind Theatre in *Griseldis*, a play written especially for her just a few years before. A crammed house greeted her in homage to her reputation as an artistic and natural actress. At the end of the piece she "was loudly called for and appeared before the curtain to again receive the plaudits of her numerous friends and admirers."[27] Such "golden accolades" were granted frequently during Mrs. Hayne's stay in Idaho City.

Julia Dean Hayne's theatrical heritage extended back to her grandfather, "Old Sam" Drake, who in 1815 at St. Louis established the first theatre west of the Mississippi. Born

Julia Dean Hayne
Utah State Historical Society
9798

in 1830, she served her acting apprenticeship in Southern and Western towns under the name of Julia Dean until her marriage to Mr. Hayne. Blessed with an exceptional beauty to accompany her histrionic talents, she became a star in the fashionable theatres of the East and a reigning favorite of the New York stage. Fleeing from an unhappy marriage, she toured to San Francisco about 1855 for an engagement and then remained in the Pacific Northwest and Rocky Mountain areas for almost twelve years, playing in Portland, Seattle, Salt Lake City and other towns from California to the Montana Territory.[28]

Mrs. Hayne's Idaho City engagement covered roughly one month to September 27, 1864. Supported by a company made up of John Potter, George Waldron, B. S. Mortimer, George Pardey, H. B. Lane, Robert Lindsay, Belle Douglas, Mr. Reeves and Mr. Robinson, she performed roles at the Jenny Lind in such well known dramas as *Romeo and Juliet, School for Scandal, Lady of Lyons, East Lynne* and *The Stranger*. She appeared four or more times in *Leah, The Forsaken, Lucretia Borgia* and *The Jewess*, roles specially suited to her talents as a tragic actress. The remainder of her performances were in the plays *The Hunchback, Masks and Faces, Fazio, Court and Siege, The Woman in White* and *The Wife's Secret*.[29]

Mrs. Hayne and most of the Potter company left for Placerville on September 27 for a brief engagement before leaving the territory to play a winter season in Portland, Oregon. Mrs. Hayne's return trip to the coast proved another perilous venture as the stage coach containing her and some of the Potter troupe turned over at Horseshoe Bend, Idaho. Fortunately she only scratched her arm and the other company members escaped unhurt.[30]

The departure of the Potter group marked the end of significant theatrical activity for 1864. George Pardey of the Potter company returned from Placerville in October to spend the winter in Idaho City and joined with Mrs. Waldron and Robert Lindsay to perform from time to time in the Jenny Lind Theatre.[31] In mid-November, Florence Bell (billed as an eminent histrionic performer from St. Louis and Denver) played a short season in *The Dead Shot, In and Out of Place* and a few other, untitled, shows.[32]

Variety and minstrel entertainment also helped pass the time during the dull winter months. Hussey's Variety Troupe arrived on October 15 and played at least two weeks at the Forrest Theatre under the management of Henry and McGinley. Led by minstrel Frank Hussey, the group featured Billy Sheppard, a jig dancer and a banjoist; Joe Mabott, ballad singer and cornet player; Mrs. Julia Morgan, danseuse, singer and general female performer; Mr. Morgan, strong man; Master Frank, India rubber boy; Lottie French, singer along with Sarah and Bobbie McGinley.[33] The company performed nightly in specialties, burlesques and "fun provoking squibs."[34] Mention of Hussey's group fails to appear in the newspaper after early November, but the names of members such as Joe Mabbot show up from time to time in various benefits held through December of 1864 and into February of 1865.

1865

Legitimate theatre did not return to Idaho City until May of 1865. As early as March 18, local businessman Fred Bell received a letter for John Potter stating Potter's intention of returning to the gold camp the first week in April.[35] In the meantime violinist John Kelly had reappeared to provide entertainments in February.[36] By late April the California Minstrels with Lew Rattler, Kelly Peel, Taylor and Sheppard tried their luck playing at Magnolia Hall. They cancelled their second night when they found audiences too small for profitable playing. The *Idaho World* tersely observed: "Money is scarce here now."[37]

After many false reports of imminent arrival, Potter and performers entered Idaho City on April 29 and began preparations for a season in the Jenny Lind Theatre one week later. Potter retained Julia Dean Hayne as his star along with supporting players George Waldron, Belle Douglas and George Pardey from the previous season and added several new performers: Mr. and Mrs. N. S. Leslie, V.A. Shields, J .H. Taylor, Mr. Graham, Miss Young, Mrs. Estelle Potter McDonald, Miss Florence Potter, Miss Belle Divine, Miss O'Keefe, Mr. Townsend, Miss Denning and Miss Sinclair.[38]

After opening on May 6, Potter and troupe presented several bills of standard favorites, *Camille*, *East Lynne*, *The Stranger*, etc., to large and presumably appreciative audiences. Encouraged by the reception of his troupe, Potter shifted his operations to the larger Forrest Theatre on May 16 where he offered an opening attraction of *The Hunchback*. The Forrest Theatre, recently improved by Mr. Henry, seated 386 and could be "crowded" to 400 in its various sections: parquette, pit, side galleries, private boxes and upper gallery.[39]

Potter's theatrical fortune rapidly turned to misfortune just two nights later (May 18) when the Forrest Theatre and much of Idaho City burned to the ground. Performers fled the theatre wearing their costumes for that night's performance of *Romeo and Juliet* and watched as the fire consumed scenery, wardrobe and personal effects. Despite losses and the emotional upsets caused by experiencing the conflagration, Potter and his troupers returned to the Jenny Lind Theatre, which had escaped damage during the fire, and on May 20 entertained patrons with *Fazio* or *The Italian Wife*.[40]

Potter's company played Idaho City for the remainder of the week, toured to Placerville for a short season and returned to present a largely new repertoire featuring several of Dion Boucicault's popular melodramas—*The Colleen Bawn*, *The Octoroon* and *Jessie Brown*— along with such standards as *Macbeth* and Boucicault's comedy of manners, *London Assurance*. Potter and his players attracted sizable audiences and enjoyed the attendant box office profits through the remainder of June without entertainment rivals save for a short engagement of the Lee and Ryland Circus on June 21.[41]

Potter's theatrical monopoly in Idaho City came to an end on July 1 with the arrival of the Selden Irwin company that began performing in the new Idaho Theatre owned by James Pinney, a man who would later play a major role in the development of theatre in Boise. Irwin's performances in the Idaho territory actually began in Boise City about June 1. About June 13 he passed through Idaho City on his way to Placerville for a week's engagement followed by another week's season at Pioneer City.[42]

Idaho City's local favorite, Sue Robinson Getzler, starred in the Irwin troupe. Mr. and Mrs. Selden Irwin played leading roles, their support supplied by the popular Robinson family (John, Clara and William) along with Charles Getzler, B. S. Mortimer, Robert Lindsay and Mrs. Waldron, the now estranged wife of George Waldron, the leading man of the rival Potter company.[43] They performed a standard repertoire of plays, many of which largely duplicated the offerings of the Potter-Hayne combination.

Through the first half of July, Idaho City theatre patrons could choose between the offerings of two active production companies, then, on July 15, the Pioneer Male and Female Minstrels arrived to further enlarge the local entertainment scene. This small minstrel troupe, made up of Johnny Edwards, Mr. and Mrs. Thomas Gibson, Mr. and Mrs. Holman and Thomas Biggs, also toured to other locales in the basin during the summer.[44]

About this time J.S. Potter decided to return to Portland and dissolved his local company. Mrs. Hayne and Waldron then formed a company consisting of Miss Belle Douglas, Mr. and Mrs. Leslie and actors Graham, Townsend, Pardey and Shields with Mr. Rosenbaum, a local business man, as treasurer. This group played four nights a week including Saturdays and Sundays at the Jenny Lind Theatre. They stayed in business for about two weeks mainly giving benefits for members of the company such as the one rendered to Mr. Potter on July 23. The press did not record the exact date of their departure from Idaho City, but by August 5 it reported that the miners missed Mrs. Hayne and "the festive throng of the Jenny Lind."[45] The August 26 *Idaho World* noted the troupe was in Salt Lake City. By 1867 Julia Dean Hayne had resumed her career in the east with somewhat less success than before her western sojourn. She remarried and in 1868 died of childbirth complications.[46] George Waldron returned to the Idaho scene in the early 1870's, then went on to forge a career that took him to New York, Chicago and other major cities in appearances with Forrest, Booth, Janauschek and other noted actors. On Broadway he played a lead role in McKee Rankin's popular Mormon epic, *The Danites*, an association which led to an appearance in that work at Sadler's Wells Theatre in London in 1880. Sometime during this London engagement he participated in a command performance before Queen Victoria. Waldron returned to America, continuing to perform in Rankin's play. He died in Waterford, New York late in 1884.[47]

After the departure of the Potter company the Irwin troupe continued productions at the Idaho Theatre through August 9 when Selden Irwin appeared in his benefit, an occasion that turned out to be a surprising and unannounced farewell performance. He hastily left town, reneging on promises to appear in fellow actors' benefits after they had dutifully performed in his. Further, according to the *Idaho World*, he committed the most scurrilous of deeds—he failed to pay his printing

Selden Irwin
Utah State Historical Society
9767

bill at the newspaper. The paper warned the residents at the site of Irwin's next engagement, Salt Lake City, that he would "bear watching."[48]

The Robinson family remained in Idaho City and presented plays for another week. By August 26 John Robinson had leased James Pinney's Idaho Theatre and announced a change in entertainment format along with a reduction in admission. His new format consisted of "Comedies, Vaudeville, Farces, Burlesques, Singing, Dancing—being what is styled VARIETIES."[49] Robinson charged fifty cents for the "pit," one dollar for the parquette and a dollar and a half for reserved seats. Occasionally he presented full-length plays such as the September 5 benefit for Mrs. MacDonald at the Jenny Lind, but Robinson drew his greatest praise from the press for presenting "pure entertainment." In the view of the *Idaho World*, "the legitimate [drama] is played out, and we want merry-making, first last and all the time."[50] Robinson's "merry-making" proved popular for only about a month. Notices of performances ceased by late September.

On September 23 the paper printed an item that brings into question the overall quality of early Idaho City theatrical presentations. After printing extravagant praises of performances every week during the theatrical season, the press printed an item that blasted performers' and producers' past efforts—at least the more recent ones. Observing that amusements had turned dull with the departure of the "theatricals," the author of the article expressed the hope that "there will be no more unless they are better."[51] Calling past entertainments "insipid," he found it "no wonder that the thing did not pay and that houses were 'only expenses.'" He further stated, "there ought to be a good company here or none." Finding that good theatre existed in the east, south and even in San Francisco, he ended his attack on Idaho City theatrical efforts by describing them as a "waste of time on good for nothing amusements at advance prices."[52]

Whether the attack on the quality of theatre in the mining camp was justified cannot be determined due to the highly personal reactions to any given theatrical presentation. Several of the major performers in Idaho City received favorable notices and attracted audiences with their talents before and after appearing in Idaho. Acting support for the stars may have been poor—a common complaint about performances in the nineteenth century. The scenic and costume resources, surely limited in so remote a location, might well detract from the quality of a production. Whatever the reason, theatre production in the mining camp had its detractors. While doubt remains as to the quality of the performances, unquestionably many in Idaho City regarded the admission price as excessive. This factor may have colored the reception of the entertainment, for the quality of performance could not have exceeded the production standards of the east, south and even San Francisco where theatres charged much less for admission.

With winter closing in on Idaho City, 1865's formal dramatic presentations ended in December when a small group consisting of Sue Robinson Getzler, Billy Robinson, Eugene Holman and others presented a few evenings of plays at the Jenny Lind Theatre. Admission cost very little and attracted full houses thus gaining the "liberal patronage" that the press had urged the citizens to give them. In spite of this success and notices of appreciation in the press that also expressed the hope they would not leave for the "barbarian burgh of Boise City,"[53] the Getzler troupe closed its short engagement after playing only December 2, 3, 9 and Christmas Day.

1866

In March and April of 1866 brief notices of entertainments at the Melodeon appeared on the pages of the *Idaho World*. Unidentified performers presented songs, dances, magic and a farce, *The Rival Tenants*.[54] True legitimate theatre did not reappear in Idaho

City until the A. R. Phelps Company, late of Walla Walla, Washington, appeared on the scene and set up shop at the Jenny Lind Theatre on May 15. Initially Fanny Morgan Phelps, Mrs. M. E. Cloud, Miss O'Keefe, I. M. Shelby, A. Redifer, J. W. Fox and the by now familiar actor, J. B. Robinson, made up the troupe. Later Eugene Holman, noted local musician, joined to provide additional entertainment between acts.[55]

After opening to a good house, "including a brilliant array of ladies,"[56] the Phelps Company sustained its attraction, playing almost every evening for ten nights to large audiences. Fanny Morgan Phelps, gifted with good enunciation and a clear, distinct, agreeable voice, rapidly became a local favorite. Mr. Phelps also made a good impression and "was greeted with constant laughter and frequent applause."[57] While some plays had the merit of being new to the territory the company's major repertoire of plays lacked innovation and tended to be mainly comic with such old standards as *The Toodles*, *The Irish Dragoon* and *Raising the Wind* relieved only with occasional performances of more dramatic works like *Charles II* and *The Stranger* or the melodrama, *Black-Eyed Susan*.

Although Phelps and his troupe had announced their plans for moving on to perform in Montana about May 26, they remained in Idaho City at the Jenny Lind long enough for Mrs. Phelps to take a complimentary benefit on June 1. At some point after her benefit Mrs. Phelps became seriously ill and did not reappear onstage until July 2. Mr. Phelps and the rest of the company, severely limited by the temporary loss of their leading lady, continued to perform during the first week in June.

On June 9 the Robinson family returned to Idaho City, leased James Pinney's Idaho Theatre and entertained sizable houses. Again, Sue Robinson Getzler starred. As the *Idaho World* observed, "She has performed in this place so long that every one knows that when he or she goes to the theatre that the scene will be one to be enjoyed."[58] "Always reliable" J. B. Robinson also earned adulation in the press for his "mimicable perfection."[59] While other actors may have appeared, notices only listed the names of performers William Robinson, George Brower and E. Rayner. By June 16, A. R. Phelps had united his talents with the Robinson company. On several occasions he served as leading man, supported by Redifer and Shelby of his now defunct troupe.[60]

Robinson's group moved its productions to the Jenny Lind Theatre sometime between June 23 and June 30 and continued to attract paying crowds to *Ingomar, the Barbarian* and other familiar favorites. On June 29 Sue Getzler took a benefit and on July 2 the now recovered Fanny Morgan Phelps appeared before a "densely crowded" theatre in her farewell benefit.[61] The evening featured performances by Sue Getzler, "unusually brilliant in her songs and dances," and the "minstrel personifications of Eugene Holman and L. Mason."[62] After the benefit, according to the press, Mrs. Phelps and her husband would make their long delayed departure for Montana on July 4, then the July 7 edition reported that they had left "this week." However, Mr. Phelps either did not accompany his wife or made a rapid round trip to Montana for his name again appears with the Robinson troupe in *Damon and Pythias* on July 21. He continued to act with this company until its season ended in Idaho City shortly after William Robinson's benefit on July 29. "Billy" Robinson, according to the press, richly deserved a benefit, his first in Idaho City, because "he has been here as long as any of them and 'played his piece' as well as the best of them."[63]

Final performances by the Robinsons at the end of July signaled the end of truly significant theatrical activity in Idaho City. Earlier, on July 7, popular violinist John Kelly and his boy, Willie were reported to be entertaining in Centerville, Hog'em, and Placerville on their way to Salt Lake City, but seemed to have bypassed Idaho City.[64] Dwyer and Kate Holman received benefits at the Melodeon on August 24 and 25. On September 8 items in the *Idaho World* commented on how quiet the town had become and how many had departed. The attraction to "The Basin Of Gold" had dimmed; miners were on their way to the next bonanza. An exhibition of a "stereoscoptican" on October 11 turned out to be the last attraction at the Jenny Lind Theatre for 1866.[65]

Except on rare occasions, acting troupes and other entertainers did not play in Idaho City after 1866. Performers lured to Silver City or passing through Boise sometimes made the side trip to the former boom town and at least one amateur troupe from Boise included Idaho City on its summer wagon tour. With its gold played out and its population of thousands reduced to only hundreds, Idaho City no longer played a significant role in the theatrical history of Idaho.

Silver City
1867-1868

Establishing early theatrical entertainment in Silver City, the site of another of Idaho's major mining booms, took several years. Prospecting parties found promising sites for gold mining in an arid mountain region some thirty miles southwest of Boise in 1863. By 1864 the town of Silver City had been established and became the center for mining, commercial and social activities. However, the first recorded instances of theatrical endeavor did not occur until September and November of 1867 in the form of reading performances by

Lisle Lester
University of Nevada, Reno
P1287

an actress, Lisle Lester, and a local amateur actor, J. Hall. Mrs. Lester performed at the Courthouse on September 27 and a Mr. Hall presented readings of the extremely popular *Lady of Lyons* at the same site on November 20 and at Orofino Hall shortly after.[66] About October 26 the Apollo Minstrels with singers Eugene and Kathy Holman and dancer Lizzie Gibson entertained for several evenings.[67]

As early as May 5, 1866 the *Owyhee Avalanche* editorial pages pointed out the need for and the advantages of building a theatre.[68] Over twenty months later, on February 8, 1868, the same paper reported on plans to erect a theatre, presumably called Hill's Theatre or Hill's Hall, on Jordan Street.[69] Exactly one month later the first acting troupe to visit Silver City had productions on the stage of the new facility.

The rather small troupe, Harry Wilkinson's Combination, featured the well known actress Charlotte Crampton, a star who was famed for playing male roles. She had enjoyed a long career acting in the East along with such notables as Edwin Booth but in her later years had been forced to make her appearances with lesser companies in often remote western towns. Nevertheless, she proved to be quite popular with the citizens of Silver City and surrounding towns, along with Lizzie Gibson, MacDonald and Harry Wilkinson. Eugene and Kitty Holman, popular entertainers earlier in Idaho City, also performed.[70]

Charlotte Crampton
Joseph Harworth Collection
www.josephharworth.com

Wilkinson's Combination played three weeks or more in a variety of plays that received favorable notice in the press, especially for productions of *Hamlet* and *Richard III*. The troupe seems to have been so limited in numbers that in a March 30 production of *Richard III*, Charlotte Crampton played Shakespeare's evil villain![71] Wilkinson's troupe seems to have left Silver City about April 20, but Miss Crampton remained until April 28 at which time she gave a program of dramatic readings as her farewell benefit.[72]

Dr. D.W. Stanley's Variety Troupe showed up in Silver City to perform on May 26. Stanley, a baritone, Sennotte, a clog and jig dancer and Gus Sprague joined with regional favorites, the Holmans, for a brief season before Stanley went back to Boise on May 28.[73]

In August of 1868 local actors formed the Silver City Amateur Theatrical Association and performed works at the Courthouse and Hill's Theatre. Their ranks included J. Hall (whose 1867 reading performances helped initiate theatre in Silver City), Ed Blake, John Graham, Robert Boyle, Louise Cable, Lizzie Usher, Lydia White and three other men. One of their major efforts was a September 5 production of *Jealous Wife* at a benefit for troupe member John Graham.[74]

Also in August of 1868, John McGinley, who had been a major figure in the earliest years of Idaho City amusements, came to Silver City and announced plans for establishing a theatre. On October 3 he opened his Owyhee Theatre on Washington Street after having played at other locations in August and September. McGinley produced works into the fall of the year and departed before the onset of winter.[75]

1869-1871

Theatre performances became rare occurrences until the spring of 1871. J. Hall presented readings in the last months of 1869 and amateurs mounted some productions in early 1869.[76] In August Miss Field appeared in readings and scenes from *Winter's Tale* and *London Assurance*.[77]

Only four theatrical events occurred in Silver City during 1870. Professor Wilkinson, a magician, gave a single performance on April 8. By May 14 the J.W. Carter company came to town and offered a season of plays, an engagement that drew the ire of the *Avalanche* editor. In the newsman's view, Carter was an ingrate for not acknowledging a free notice and a miser for not having his printing done locally. In addition, the paper printed a Boise City item alleging that Carter had forced a sick actress from her bed and made her perform in spite of her illness. For this Carter earned the dubious accolades of "brute" and "puppy" from the press.[78] For obvious reasons, the Carter season ended quite early in Silver City.

Months passed before Bartholemew's Lilliputian Circus arrived in town on September 12 to offer a performance in a tent pitched near the Idaho Saloon. The circus with its trained ponies and goats returned to Silver City twelve days later for two more shows before leaving for Boise.[79] The last of a limited year of entertainments took place at Hill's Hall on December 31 with an amateur benefit presentation of *Love and Luck*, a local drama written by one Henry Martin.[80]

In 1871 Silver City's citizenry enjoyed a relatively active theatrical calendar. Father Poulon organized a community concert for March 17 at Hill's Hall.[81] By May 6 of that year the Carrie Chapman troupe reached Silver City and opened for business. This small troupe of Carrie Chapman, Mr. McCarty, William Etherton and Clara Lewis stayed for at least two weeks.[82]

In late July the Pixley sisters, Annie and Minnie, under the management of Ned Campbell, came to Silver City from Boise.[83] While the sisters, especially Annie, later became nationally recognized performers, at

Annie Pixley
University of Washington
Libraries Special Collections
S-P-271

23

this point in their careers they were still in need of honing their skills in acting, dancing as well as singing. Beginning as child entertainers in Olympia, Washington, they had toured extensively in Washington, Oregon and British Columbia before entering the Idaho Territory.[84] Their Silver City company included William Etherton and Clara Lewis from the Chapman troupe and local amateur, J. Hall. They entertained at Hill's Theatre for a week presenting works such as *Charles II, The Colleen Bawn* and *Caste* before returning to Boise about the first of August.[85]

The Holmans, Billy Wilkinson and Frank Sparrow played in nearby towns between mid-July and mid-August before performing in Silver City itself on July 17 and August 19. Wilkinson specialized in rope tying feats, Eugene Holman danced a "champion jig" and Mrs. Holman sang the latest ballads.[86]

The Nathan troupe became the last troupe to perform in Silver City during 1871. The unique, all juvenile, troupe, under the management of Mr. Vincent, had already played other towns in the Boise Basin. The local press favored "Little Marion," but failed to note her roles or even mention the titles of the Nathan Company's shows. After a short season the "little troupers" toured onward toward the East, the press reporting later their proposed engagement in St. Louis.[87]

1872-1875

Not a single professional troupe seems to have even approached Silver City in 1872. 1873 almost became an equally empty theatrical year except for two weeks of performances by the George Waldron Company during the first part of June. Waldron, a key figure in the earlier theatre of Idaho City, had gained further acting and managerial experience in Montana and Colorado before returning to establish a base in Portland, Oregon. His Silver City season followed a short Boise engagement in late May and early June.

His eight person company profited well during the Silver City stay, fulfilling a manager's dream—playing to several full houses.[88]

In December of 1873 the *Avalanche* reported some form of dramatic presentations being given at Champion Hall, a new theatre facility with an outside stairway leading up to its location on the second story of the Granite Block. This theatre, with an estimated seating capacity of 150 or more, provided a home for productions of the Silver City Dramatic Association in February of 1874 and of the visiting Rosedale Troupe in June of the same year. The dramatic association's opening performance on February 14 provided unexpected thrills when a supporting timber of the building settled, setting off a short lived panic in the assembly.[89]

The Rosedale Troupe had to provide its own thrills at Champion Hall. Arriving in June of 1874, this company performed in Silver City and nearby Fairview for one of the longest seasons in the area, twenty-two nights.[90] Featured players, Mr. and Mrs. Fulford (the former Annie Pixley), made a hit, especially her impersonations and her special singing number, "Chin Chow Chow."[91]

Like Idaho City before, the mining activity in and around Silver City diminished and with it died the attraction for professional troupes. Even before the Rosedale Troupe came to town the paper reported that the old Silver City Theatre (possibly Hill's Theatre or McGinley's Owyhee Theatre) would be destroyed for materials to build a new engine house.[92] Although visits by professional troupes became even rarer as the years passed, some amateur productions appeared from time to time. In February and March of 1876 the Silver City Dramatic Association, under the leadership of a Professor Butler, put together productions of *The Stranger* and *Slasher and Crasher*. By late March and early April the group had added *Chimney Corner*, *Betsy Blake*, *The Toodles* and *The Live Woman in the Mines* to its repertoire. The association of amateurs toured all of these shows to Boise and other towns in the basin where they attracted sizable audiences and the regard of the press that viewed them as better than the professional acting companies which sometimes visited the mountain towns. In addition to Professor Butler, who directed and played the leading man roles, the company included Miss Ada Leigh as leading lady, Patton as comedian and Mr. and Mrs. A. Bomar. Professor H. L. Gates provided music.[93]

As amateurs helped to begin theatre in Silver City, they played their parts in bringing significant performing activity to a close. Slowly Silver City became a ghost town that troupers passed by on the north and south.

Boise City
1864

In 1864, when the theatrical history of Boise City began, the future state capital of Idaho served mainly as a supply station for the Boise Basin mining camps. Like the camps it served, it existed far from other population centers. Salt Lake City could be reached in four days in a most uncomfortable Overland Stage, Denver in ten. Portland lay some days remote to the west. As it did everything else, the factor of isolation affected the development of theatre in Boise for a score of years after the first plays opened in a Boise saloon.

Boise's first entertainment, Dan Rice's Circus (managed by William T. Ayman), pitched its tent for a two day stay on August 5 of 1864. The Rice aggregation carried few performers. Ayman, described as a "celebrated" clown, doubled as a "general performer." William Franklin appeared as a "great Sommersault rider and principal equestrian," with Messrs. Durand and Painteras "Champion gymnasts and Acrobats." Notices emphasized "Single and Double acts of horsemanship, Daring break-neck acts, Terrific feats of vaulting, Trick horses," and Pete and Barney, "Educated mules."[94] W.C. Smith served as advance agent and Max Zwa as band leader. M'lle Emma also performed in some unnamed specialty. The *Idaho*

Tri-Weekly Statesman commented on the pioneer circus effort—reporting that the group played "to a full pavillion" and "well sustained reputation as first class acrobats and gymnasts."[95] As Ayman's circus departed to play mining towns in the basin during August, the paper urged the support of this pioneer effort to bring entertainment to the new territory.

The distinction of being the first individual to present *dramatic* entertainments in Boise fell to the widely traveled, veteran actor-manager, John S. Potter, who had brought a theatrical company to Idaho City earlier in 1864. After playing in Idaho City for some months, Potter brought his company to Boise on August 10. The next day he temporarily converted the Idaho Saloon into the Idaho Theatre and that evening presented a double bill of *The Lady of Lyons* and *The Lottery Ticket* plus assorted songs and dances. Notices for the performance listed the company for that night as follows: the favorite young tragedian, George B. Waldron; the popular comic actor, George Pardey; the celebrated vocalist, R. H. Lindsay; the popular tragedian, J. B. Smith; the light comedian, J. Messenger; the favorite actress, Miss Belle Douglas; the popular comic actress, Mrs. Waldron; the popular danseuse, Mrs. E. Pemberton; and the veteran actor, John S. Potter. Mr. N. Barney provided music.[96]

On the occasion the *Statesman* wrote: "As this will be the first night in our city of a theatre of any sort, the talented company will undoubtedly take their bows before a crowded house."[97] Potter and his company did indeed experience good houses for the opening night and for the two other nights of their extremely brief season. The bill for August 12 went unreported in the press, but on August 13 George Waldron and Belle Douglas starred in the often produced *Ingomar, the Barbarian.* After his short stay in Boise, Potter returned with his company to Idaho City where he added Julia Dean Hayne as his star and played through late September.

After a taste of dramatic entertainment, variety performers provided the few other diversions listed for 1864 in Boise. On August 23 the *Statesman* reported that "After considerable labor and expense," Billy Sheppard "organized a talented troupe of male and female performers under the name of [the] 'Congo Minstrels.'"[98] The "talented troupe" of locals consisted of L. Moulton, Miss Sue Moulton, Tom Briggs, Sheppard, Barry and "other good deliniators, singers and dancers" who performed in the Idaho Saloon up to at least October 15.[99] Although primarily variety performers, they did present at least one short farce, *The Ebony Statue,* as part of their bill on September 17. On October 4 and 12 the well known and popular violinist, John and Will Kelly, gave performances at the Overland Hotel and attracted a "hall filled to overflowing."[100] The Kellys joined with the Congo Minstrels for a performance on October 15 that included a "burlesque opera" entitled *The Virginia Cupids* with Kelly in the "laughable character of 'Cuff'" and Miss Sue Moulton as "Rose Peachblossom."[101] Kelly and Willie concluded their visit to Boise with a final show on October 19 at the Overland. Prof. Myers, the magician who established the Magic Temple in Idaho City, also performed feats of magic, legerdemain and trickery under the title of *A Night in Wonderland* at the Overland just two days earlier.[102]

1865

Regular dramatic productions did not return to Boise until the summer of 1865 when two troupes presented seasons for Boise residents. Until that time variety performers Gibson, Holman and Moulton provided entertainments at Huggin's Hall in January and at the Overland Hotel in April.[103]

Boise's entertainment drought came to an end on June 6 with the arrival of the Irwin-Getzler theatrical combination made up of actors from the Selden Irwin troupe and the well known Robinson company with Sue Robinson Getzler. The group, on its way to play gold camps in the Boise Basin, stopped off for a short season of five performances at an unspecified location that, according to the *Statesman* of June 8, had poor conditions for playing, "lacking all the scenery and appointments of a regular theatre."[104] In spite of the physical limitations of its "theatre," the company earned repeated applause from crowded houses during their June 6 presentation of *Betsy Blake* and *In and Out of Place* and its June 7 rendering of *The Colleen Bawn*. The troupe continued its success with *Honeymoon* and *Fool of the Family* on the eighth, *The Octoroon* on the ninth and a concluding bill of *Our American Cousin* and *Nan, the Good For Nothing*, on the tenth. Reviews of productions contained flattering praise for individual actors and singled out Mrs. Irwin and Sue Getzler for their histrionic excellence.[105] Following the Irwin-Getzler appearances, a variety group called The California Minstrels came to Boise from Idaho City to present two "Grand Parlor Entertainments" on June 13 and 14.[106] Tommy Pell, Henry Williams, Joe Mabbott, Joe Taylor and Mat Kelly performed the songs, dances and jokes developed during their stay in the mining camps. Lee and Ryland's Grand Combination Circus finally reached Boise for two shows on June 15. Although advertised to reach town earlier, the circus missed original dates due to loss of stock. A two dollar fee admitted Boiseans to witness the skill of J. B. Rochette and his dog and monkey show.[107]

The George Waldron troupe with star Julia Dean Hayne became the second theatrical group to try its fortune in Boise during the summer of 1865. Notices of the company's intention to play on July 22 appeared in the press on July 15 but actual performances did not begin until July 25 due to delayed arrival of the company's baggage. While the *Statesman* failed to report the bill for the first night and the performance site for the entire season, it did reveal that Mrs. Hayne attracted a full house on opening night and for her performance in *Camille* on the twenty-sixth. Mrs. Hayne and the

Waldron company presented *The Lady of Lyons* on June 27 followed by *Leah* (one of Mrs. Hayne's most noted roles) on the following evening. On July 29 the company offered a combination of serious melodrama and "roaring farce," *The Stranger* and *Pocahantas*.[108] The title of the troupe's final production on July 31 did not appear in the press. Waldron's troupe seems to have split up after the brief Boise season with some players returning to Idaho City and some others going to Portland.

Except for a farewell benefit by John Kelly at Sanderson's Hall on September 9, Boise citizens had been without the delights of "theatricals" for six weeks when the Robinson troupe returned to Boise on September 13 to play a ten day engagement.[109] Titles of Robinson's productions at Sanderson Hall failed to appear in the press except those of *Naval Engagements* and *The Swiss Swain*, produced on September 16. The troupe did receive favorable notices such as a "little company with superior talent" being "fully appreciated" and experiencing "unparalleled success" in drawing crowded houses.[110] Items listed members of the company as Sue Getzler, Mr. and Mrs. Lindsay, Clara Robinson and J. B. Robinson. The company departed for parts unknown at the end of the season in September but returned in the dead of winter on December 28 to open the first extended theatrical season in Boise.

1866

During 1866 Boise's inhabitants witnessed more plays than had been offered in any previous season. The Robinson family presented most of them in Sanderson Hall in a season that lasted from January 1 to early May. The company of about eight made up of the Robinsons, the Getzlers, Mrs. Lindsay and Robert Lindsay (a former member of John Kelly's minstrel organization), presented a limited repertory of plays with modest sized casts. For some performances locals Bill Robertson, J. L. Hall and George Brower performed in specialty numbers. The troupe did not play nightly but averaged three performances a week with several cancellations due to severe weather conditions and one due to the serious illness of Mrs. Getzler. The company gave the usual benefits for individual actors as well as some for local charity efforts such as the February 27 performance for the Volunteer Fund that cleared $175 for the organization.[111]

The *Idaho Tri-Weekly Statesman* championed the efforts of the Robinsons, lauding the talents of "the dashing Mrs. Sue Robinson Getzler" and her "faultless acting, charming singing and graceful dancing."[112] In an attempt at editorial cleverness the March 15 *Statesman* reported that the performance of *Kill or Cure* and *Family Jars* on March 17 would be free, "except that Brother Robinson will take up a small collection at the door just to pay the revenue tax, say a dollar or a dollar and a half."[113] On March 24 the paper requested a good turn-out for Charles Getzler's benefit for "Mr. Getzler has been at a great deal of expense and trouble and overcame great obstacles in affording us amusement during the winter."[114] This request produced a house "filled to overflowing."[115]

After the April 7 performance of *Naval Engagements* and *The Little Savage* the Robinson family's long season at Sanderson Hall halted for two weeks, resuming at the same site under the management of William H. Robinson who re-opened the theatre as a "treat" to citizens.[116] By May 5 the season came to a complete end with a final bill of *The Two Bonnycastles* and *The Hermit.*

Three days after the curtain finally came down on the Robinson family's four month season, A.R. Phelps' troupe, on its way to Idaho City, stopped and played a four day engagement in Boise. The May 8 paper noted that local residents already knew several members of the company and that, without insult to the departed Robinson family, it was nice "to see new faces on the boards."[117] Fanny Morgan Phelps, a "well known and favorite actress" who had travelled in Australia, British Columbia, California and Oregon, starred in her "celebrated Irish and Scotch characters."[118]   Phelps offered plays from the same rather standard repertoire he later presented in Idaho City, *The Stranger*, *The Lady of Lyons*, *The Toodles*, etc.

The remainder of the entertainment calendar for Boise in 1866 amounted to an alternation of appearances by John Kelly and the Robinson-Getzler combination. Kelly and, of course, Willie Kelly gave concerts on May 24, May 31 and June 11. The Robinson troupe stopped at Boise between its tours to Idaho City and other regional mining camps, playing a season in Boise between May 26 and June 2 and then returning with Mr. and Mrs. Phelps to offer a four-night engagement that commenced on August 8.[119]

For these two engagements the Robinsons established the Ada Theatre in a new building opposite Biliche and Logan's Store. Reportedly Mr. Getzler "spared no pains in providing the most comfortable and convenient theatre this side of Portland."[120] Additional room in the new location enabled the troupe to present "more select and better style plays than before."[121]   While the Robinson-Getzler company continued to present some all too familiar works such as *Ingomar* and *Damon and Pythias*, they did offer a few plays like *Maid of Croissey* and *Dead Shot* that, while not new in the repertoire of American stock companies, were new to Boise.

1867

After the August, 1866 performances by the Robinsons, the *Statesman* did not mention any theatrical amusements until the single appearance of a magician named Dodds at Hart's Hall (located on Seventh and Idaho) on July 23, 1867.[122] Understandably, this dearth of amusements in Boise coincided with the decline in Boise Basin mining activity, there being fewer people and, more importantly, fewer dollars to attract touring stock companies to the area. In the entire year of 1867 only six individuals or groups came to Boise, presenting a total of just sixteen performances.

Dodds, the magician who had given the season's first show returned to Boise on November 26, 1867 as the last attraction of the year.[123] In between his engagements several entertainers visited Boise. Two minstrel groups offered shows: The Montana Minstrels on September 7 and the Apollo Minstrels on October 7 through 9.[124] The latter group came from Idaho City and featured the locally well recognized talents of Chapman, Mrs. Eugene Holman, Ward and Mr. and Mrs. T. Gibson. Mrs. Lisle Lester, elocutionist, also appeared, offering dramatic readings on September 24 and October 7.[125]

After travelling 400 miles from Montana in a trip that wore out men and horses, Bartholemew's Great Western Circus drew a $1,000 house in Boise on September 10. Following a second performance the circus left to play in Idaho City and other mining camps before returning to Boise for shows on October 1 and 3.[126]

Two nights later, Charlotte Crampton gave scenes and dramatic readings at Hart's Hall, performances repeated on October 12, 14 and 26. The Fort Boise Glee Club appeared with her on one occasion and she may have enlisted the aid of some amateurs to assist in her scenes from *Hamlet* and *Lucretia Borgia*. Reportedly after her last show in October she put together a "select little company" for a tour to Idaho City.[127] Over a year later, on July 13, 1869, the editor of the *Statesman*, after reporting on Charlotte Crampton's activities in Kansas, added the unkind comment that her group not only owed him thirty dollars, but that "they are a set of drunken bumming bilks."[128]

1868

Even fewer entertainers came to Boise during 1868 and none of them presented dramatic performances of any type. The

Statesman carried notices describing Dr. D. W. Stanley's Variety troupe and its shows at Hart's Hall (also called Hart's Exchange) in late April and part of May. Stanley and his company had performed in California and Oregon before arriving in Boise. Besides Dr. Stanley, Wilkinson's name

Hart's Hall or Exchange
Idaho State Historical Society
2111

showed up in print as a member of the company during its first engagement. After performing from April 21 through 23, the company left to try its luck in the Idaho City area. Stanley's company returned for two shows later in May having added to its ranks the popular local musicians from Idaho City, Mr. and Mrs. Eugene Holman. Stanley took his troupe right back to Idaho City after his final show on May 30.[129]

On July 28 Mr. and Mrs. Bob McGinley, who had been a part of the Boise Basin theatrical scene almost from its beginnings, came to Boise to play two nights at Hart's Hall before continuing onto Silver City.[130] The sparse diversions for 1868 ended on August 8 when Martin, the Wizard completed a four-night season of magic at Hart's Hall.[131]

1869

The number of shows presented for Boise's inhabitants in 1869 increased only slightly with local amateur groups furnishing most of them. The *Statesman* reported absolutely nothing about performances in Boise for almost ten months. Then, the very talented, and equally eccentric, George Pauncefort presented a program of readings from Charles Dickens on June 18 and 23 at Hart's Hall.[132]

George Pauncefort, a well recognized talent from the English stage in his youth, emigrated to America where he repeated his success in New York before seeking the challenge and adventure of playing in the West, first with John Langrishe's company in Denver during the Colorado gold rush and then in the Montana territory. He may also have been escaping from marital discord and certain misunderstandings with several women. Whatever the reason for being in the west, Pauncefort enjoyed his life in the sparsely settled regions of the Pacific Northwest. Area

George Pauncefort
University of Utah,
J. Willard Marriott Library
P0001G078

newspapers, including the *Statesman*, printed long articles authored by Pauncefort that extolled the wonders of his favorite pastimes, fishing and riding horses. Eventually Pauncefort worked his way to California, performing in communities of all sizes. Ever the wanderer, he sailed to Asia, fought pirates near Formosa, opened a restaurant in Japan and acted with Japanese Noh drama artists.[133]

Pauncefort's efforts at presenting Dickens to the Boise public in June met with "sterling success" and resulted in full houses where patrons' shouts of laughter rang through the hall as they listened to readings from *Pickwick Papers* and *Nicholas Nickleby*.[134] Pauncefort again brought his Dickens program to Hart's Hall on September 15 and 21, this time adding scenes from *David Copperfield* to his bill.[135]

Professor Hermann and Miss M. Field presented the only other professional entertainment in Boise for 1869. Hermann amused patrons with his magic show and ventriloquist act on June

26.[136] Miss Field displayed her elocutionary skills at a reading on August 7 at Hart's Hall.[137]

What few other entertainments graced the year came from the efforts of amateur groups, civilian and military. Local residents put together a "Parlor Theatrical Entertainment" at Slocum's Hall as a benefit for the Citizen's Cemetery Fund on August 5, the entertainment consisting of two plays, *The Widow's Victim* and *Betsy Blake*.[138] In addition to this single production by Boise residents in 1869, the "boys in blue" from the garrison at Fort Boise exhibited their talents no less than four times before the year ended.

Fort Boise had been established in 1863 mainly as a base for campaigns against the native American tribes. With time on their hands between missions, members of the garrison relieved the boredom of military routine by rehearsing and presenting public entertainments. On August 31, 1869 the soldiers announced their intentions of forming a minstrel band to "give public entertainments from time to time."[139] The Fort Boise Minstrels, as they came to be known, boasted ten members who played such instruments as banjo, bones, violin and triangle. They performed in a cavalry barracks fitted up as a performance hall.[140]

The Fort Boise minstrels presented their first entertainment in their converted barracks theatre on September 4 and followed with another show on September 10. Soldiers not only provided welcome diversions for Boise residents, they also furnished transportation to the fort from Hart's Exchange and the hotel in a military ambulance. They produced a new bill of variety acts on October 15 and 21 including a short farce, *The Black Statue*. For their final effort on December 15 and 18, the Fort Boise Varieties, as they now titled themselves, enlisted the aid of three talented Boise women (Mrs. Evans, Mrs. Agnew and Mrs. Brown) to appear in the production at the Fort Boise hall.[141]

During the first seven years of theatre in the Boise Basin, the dramatic events of the gold rush and the attendant explosion of growth in the region all but eclipsed the traditional dramatic action on the stage. Still the sons and daughters of Thespis had played parts on stage and off to inform and influence this early society. They served as a reminder of the life left behind, symbolic of a remote, more comfortable way of living. For an evening they diverted thoughts away from the harshness and loneliness of mining camp life. Even the shabby, "cheap penny" troupes could lend an air of elegance to town life and offer escape from tedium and routine.

CHAPTER 1 NOTES

1   *Boise News* (Idaho City), October 13, 1863, p. 3.

2   *Ibid.*, November 10, 1863, p. 2; November 28, 1863, p. 2; December 5, 1863, p. 4.

3   *Ibid.*, May 7, 1864, p. 2.

4   *Ibid.*, December 12, 1863, p. 2; January 23, 1864, p. 3.

5   *Ibid.*, December 26, 1863, p. 4.

6   *Ibid.*, January 9, 1864, p. 2; February 6, 1864, p. 2; February 20, 1864, p. 2.

7   *Ibid.*, March 5, 1864, p. 2.

8   *Ibid.*

9   *Ibid.*, January 30, 1864.

10 *Ibid.*, April 9, 1864, p. 2; April 16, 1864, p. 2; April 23, 1864, p. 2.

11 *Ibid.*, March 19, 1864, p. 2.

12 *Ibid.*, April 23, 1864, p. 2.

13 *Ibid.*, May 7, 1864, p. 2.

14 *Ibid.*, April 30, 1864, p. 2; May 7, 1864, p. 2.

15 Sol Smith, *Theatrical Management* (New York: Benjamin Blom, Inc., 1968), p. 232. Reprint of 1868 edition.

16 Margaret G. Watson, *Silver Theatre: Amusements of Nevada's Mining Frontier*, 1850-1864 (Glendale, California: Arthur H. Clark Company,1964), pp.8-9.

17 *Boise News* (Idaho City), May 7, 1864, p. 2.

18 *Ibid.*

19 *Ibid.*

20 *Ibid.*, May 28, 1864, p. 2.

21 *Ibid.*

22 Lyle Schwarz, "Theatre On The Gold Frontier: A Cultural Study of Five Northwest Towns" (Ph.D. diss., Washington State University, 1975), p. 91. There is some discrepancy in her death date. The *Idaho Tri-Weekly Statesman* (Boise) reported her death in the June 22, 1871 edition, p. 3.

23 *New York Mirror*, February 2, 1884, p. 3

24 *Boise News*, (Idaho City), June 4, 1864, p. 2.

25 *Ibid.*, June 11, 1864, p. 3.

26 *Ibid.*, August 27, 1864, p. 3.

27 *Ibid.*, September 3, 1864, p. 2.

28 Lloyd Morris, *Curtain Time* (New York: Random House, 1953), p. 144; Phylliss Hartnoll, ed., *The Oxford Companion to the Theatre*, 2nd ed. *(London: Oxford University Press, 1957, p. 190.*

29 *Boise News*, September 3, 1864, p.2; September 10, 1864, p. 2; September 17, 1864, p. 2; September 24, 1864, p. 2.

30 *Ibid.*, October 15, 1864, p. 3.

31 *Ibid.*, October 1, 1864, p. 2; October 8, 1864, p. 2; October 15, 1864, p. 2; *Idaho World* (Idaho City), November 5, 1864, p. 3.

32 *Idaho World* (Idaho City), November 12, 1864, p. 2.

33 *Ibid.*, October 22, 1864, p. 2; November 5, 1864, p. 3.

34 *Ibid.*, November 5, 1864, p. 3.

35 *Ibid.*, March 18, 1865, p. 3.

36 *Ibid.*, February 11, 1865, p. 3.

37 *Ibid.*, April 22, 1865, p. 3; April 29, 1865, p. 2.

38 *Ibid.*, March 18, 1865, p. 3; May 3, 1865, p. 3.

39 *Ibid.*, May 6, 1865, p. 2; May 13, 1865, p. 2.

40 *Ibid.*, May 20, 1865, pp. 2, 3.

41 *Ibid.*, May 27, 1865, p. 3; June 3, 1865, p. 3; June 10, 1865, p. 3; June 17, 1865, p. 2; June 24, 1865, p. 2; July 1, 1865, pp. 2,3.

42 *Ibid.*, June 17, 1865, p. 2; June 24, 1865, pp. 2, 3; July 1, 1865, p. 2.

43 *Ibid.*, July 8, 1865, p. 2.

44 *Ibid.*, July 15, 1865, p. 3.

45 *Ibid.*, August 5, 1865, p. 2.

46 Hartnoll, p. 190.

47 *New York Mirror*, February 2, 1884, p. 3.

48 *Idaho World*, August 19, 1865, p. 2.

49 *Ibid.*, August 26, 1865, p. 2.

50 *Ibid.*, September 2, 1865, p. 3.

51 *Ibid.*, September 23, 1865, p. 3.

52 *Ibid.*

53 *Ibid.*, December 23, 1865, p. 3.

54 *Ibid.*, March 31, 1866, p. 3.

55 *Ibid.*, May 19, 1866, p. 3; May 26, 1866, p. 2.

56 *Ibid.*, May 19, 1866, p. 3.

57 *Ibid.*

58 *Ibid.*, June 16, 1866, p. 3.

59 *Ibid.*

60 *Ibid.*

61 *Ibid.*, July 7, 1866, p. 3.

62 *Ibid.*

63   *Ibid.*, July 28, 1866, p. 3.

64   *Ibid.*, July 7, 1866, p. 3.

65   *Ibid.*, August 4, 1866, p. 3; August 25, 1866, p. 3; September 8, 1866, p. 3; October 13, 1866, p. 3.

66   *Owyhee Avalanche* (Silver City), September 14, 1867, p. 3; October 17, 1867, p. 3; November 16, 1867, p. 3; November 30, 1867, p. 3.

67   *Ibid.*, October 26, 1867, p. 3.

68   *Ibid.*, May 5, 1866, p. 3. At this time the paper was printed in Ruby City, a town a mile from Silver City.

69   *Ibid.*, October 26, 1868, p. 3.

70   *Ibid.*, February 22, 1868, p. 3; February 29, 1868, p. 2; March 7, 1868, p. 3.

71   *Ibid.*, April 4, 1868, p. 2.

72   *Ibid.*, April 26, 1868, p. 3.

73   *Ibid.*, May 23, 1868, p. 3; May 30, 1868, p. 3.

74   Fred Gilliard, "Early Theater In The Owyhees," *Idaho Yesterdays* (Summer, 1973), 17/2:112.

75   *Owyhee Avalanche*, August 1, 1868, p. 3; August 15, 1868, p. 3; September 5, 1868, p. 2; September 12, 1868, p. 3; October 3, 1868, p. 2; October 17, 1868, p. 2; November 7, 1868, p. 3; December 5, 1868, p. 2.

76   *Ibid.*, January 9, 1869, p3; January 23, 1869, p. 3; February 6, 1869, p. 3; February 13, 1869, p. 3; February 27, 1869, p. 3; March 13, 1869, p. 3; May 8, 1869, p. 3.

77   *Ibid.*, August 23, 1869, p. 3.

78   *Ibid.*, May 21, 1870.

79   *Ibid.*, September 13, 1870, p. 3; September 24, 1870, p. 3.

80   *Ibid.*, December 31, 1870, p. 3.

81   *Ibid.*, March 25, 1871, p. 2.

82   *Ibid.*, April 29, 1871, p. 3; May 6, 1871, p. 2.

83   *Ibid.*, July 18, 1871, p. 3.

84   Alice Henson Ernst, *Trouping In the Oregon Country* (Portland, Oregon: Oregon Historical Society, 1961), p. 53.

85   *Owyhee Avalanche*, July 22, 1871, p. 3; July 29, 1871, p. 2.

86   *Ibid.*, July 22, 1871, p. 3; August 19, 1871, p. 3.

87   *Ibid.*, November 25, 1871, p. 2 and 3; December 2, 1871, p.3.

88   Gilliard, p. 14.

89   *Ibid.*, p.15.

90   *Ibid.*

91   *Owyhee Avalanche*, June 6, 1874, p. 2.

92   *Ibid.*, May 2, 1874, p. 3.

93   *Ibid.*, February 19, 1876 p. 3; February 26, 1876, p. 3; April 8, 1876, p. 4.

94   *Idaho Tri-Weekly Statesman* (Boise), August 4, 1864, p. 2.

95   *Ibid.*, August 9, 1864, p. 2.

96   *Ibid.*, August 11, 1864, p. 2.

97   *Ibid.*

98   *Ibid.*, August 23, 1864, p. 2.

99   *Ibid.*, September 13, 1864, p. 2; September 20, 1864, p. 2; October, 17, 1864, p. 2.

100   *Ibid.*, October 6, 1864, p. 3; October 13, 1864, p. 2.

101   *Ibid.*, October 15, 1864, p. 2.

102   *Ibid.*, October 18, 1864, p. 2.

103   *Ibid.*, January 7, 1865, p. 2; January 14, 1865, p. 2; April 25, 1865, p. 2.

104   *Ibid.*, June 8, 1865, p. 2.

105   *Ibid.*, June 8, 1865, p. 2; June 10, 1865, p. 2.

106   *Ibid.*, June 13, 1865, p. 2.

107   *Ibid.*, June 8, 1865, p. 2; June 15, 1865, p. 2.

108   *Ibid.*, July 25, 1865, p. 2; July 27, 1865, p. 2; July 29, 1865, p. 2.

109   *Ibid.*, September 7, 1865, p. 2; September 14, 1865, p. 2.

110   *Ibid.*, September 14, 1865, p. 2; September 19, 1865, p. 2.

111   *Ibid.*, February 27, 1865, p. 2.

112   *Ibid.*, January 2, 1866, p. 2.

113   *Ibid.*, March 15, 1866, p. 2.

114   *Ibid.*, March 24, 1866, p. 2.

115   *Ibid.*, March 29, 1866, p. 2.

116   *Ibid.*, April 21, 1866, p. 2.

117   *Ibid.*, May 8, 1866, p. 2.

118   *Ibid.*, May 12, 1866, p. 2.

119   *Ibid.*, May 26, 1866, p. 3; May 29, 1866, p. 2; June 2, 1866, p. 2; August 7, 1866, p. 2, August 11, 1866, p. 4.

120   *Ibid.*, May 26, 1866, p. 3.

121   *Ibid.*, May 29, 1866, p. 2.

122   *Ibid.*, July 23, 1867, p. 3.

123   *Ibid.*, November 26, 1867, p. 2.

124   *Ibid.*, September 7, 1867, p. 3; October 5, 1867, p. 2; October 8, 1867, p. 3.

125   *Ibid.*, September 26, 1867, p. 3; October 5, 1867, p. 2.

126   *Ibid.*, September 12, 1867; October 1, 1867, p. 3.

127   *Ibid.*, October 1, 1867, p. 3; October 5, 1867, p. 3 October 12, 1867, p. 3; October 15, 1867, p. 3; October 26, 1867, p. 3.

128   *Ibid.*, July 13, 1869, p. 3.

129   *Ibid.*, April 21, 1868, p. 3; April 23, 1868, p. 3; April 25, 1868, p. 3; May 28, 1868, p. 3; May 30, 1868, p. 3.

130   *Ibid.*, July 28, 1868, p. 3; July 30, 1868, p. 3.

131   *Ibid.*, August 6, 1868, p. 2.

132   *Ibid.*, June 17, 1869, p. 1; June 24, 1869, p. 3.

133   Melvin Schoberlin, *From Candles to Footlights* (Denver: The Old West Publishing Co., 1941), pp. 113, 114, 282.

134   *Idaho Tri-Weekly Statesman*, June 19, 1869, p. 3; June 24, 1869, p.3.

135   *Ibid.*, September 14, 1869, p. 3; September 18, 1869, p. 3; September 21, 1869, p. 3.

136   *Ibid.*, June 26, 1869, p. 3.

137   *Ibid.*, August 10, 1869, p. 2.

138   *Ibid.*, August 5, 1869, p. 3.

139   *Ibid.*, August 31, 1869, p. 3.

140   *Ibid.*

141   *Ibid.*, September 7, 1869, p. 3; September 9, 1869, p. 3; October 14, 1869, p. 3; October 21, 1869, p. 3; December 14, 1869, p. 3.

CHAPTER 2

The Lean Years

Boise, Idaho: 1870-1879

Idaho lacked a connection with a transcontinental railroad system to link its few major towns until 1883, thus the southwest part of the territory especially failed to share in the abundance of various entertainments available to most Americans. While others feasted from a large menu of diversions, Boise's citizens experienced lean years for amusement in the 1870's. Entertainment did not cease altogether and, in spite of remoteness and some hard times, amateurs still joined together to amuse their fellow citizens. Occasionally professional entertainers braved stagecoach or wagon travel to try their luck before a new public.

1870

After the dearth of amusements in the seasons of 1868 and 1869, the Boise public experienced what must have seemed a flood of diversions in 1870 when over twenty-five evenings of various entertainments were offered. No less than three magicians conjured for the mystification of Boise audiences. Professor Wilkinson, a very pleasing performer, puzzled spectators, first at Hart's Hall on February 26 and at Good Templars Hall (near the corner of Sixth and Main) on February 28, with his African ball trick.[142] The Great Maximillian followed at Good Templars Hall on April 5,6,7 and Professor Hermann renewed his acquaintance with local residents on October 7 and 8 at the same hall.[143] A popular "elocutionist," Professor C. B. Plummer, gave his readings at Good Templars Hall on June 10 and August 13.[144] Bartholemew's Lilliputian Circus erected its tent on a vacant lot north of the Episcopal Church on

September 3 for a three show engagement featuring "acrobats, contortionists, trick ponies and trained goats."[145] Boise amateurs filled in with a concert on February 8 at Slocum's Hall and an untitled entertainment on April 14.[146]

Boise's Judge Robert L. Gillespie directed a local amateur group that presented plays at Good Templars Hall in October and November of 1870. The *Statesman* listed Gillespie as "stage

Good Templars Hall
Idaho State Historical Society
964

manager" and a Mr. Richardson acted as treasurer for the October 22 bill of *Family Jars* and *Nan, The Good For Nothing*. Newspaper notices listed a Mrs. Minnie Chapman along with the other performers: Mr. Charles Graham, Jones, H. McNeilly, Master Robert Gillespie jr., Miss Clark Lewis and R. Mobley. Their production "gave satisfaction to a large audience" and, although the performers "labored under many difficulties in giving their first appearance," it "was a creditable one."[147] On November 17 Gillespie's thespians gave *Still Waters Run Deep* as their second and last show in Boise. In addition to the players in the first production Clifford, Schwatka, Samuels and Mary Chapman joined the company for this effort. Two nights later Boise Thespians tendered Judge Gillespie a benefit for "his efforts to offer popular entertainments this winter."[148]

Two professional theatre companies provided the remainder of the entertainment offerings for 1870. First came the Carter troupe on April 16, the first professional dramatic troupe to visit Idaho in several years. After playing in Boise for a week, they made a tour of mining camps in the basin and then returned to Boise about May 8 for a brief season before leaving for the Owyhees on May 13. Posted show bills touted the arrival of the leading lady Miss Carrie Carter and a full supporting company. Only the names of Carter, Mr. and Mrs. Lipsis and Patton appeared in reviews of the company's shows. A local man, Wilkinson (perhaps Professor Wilkinson, the magician), acted a role in *Camille*.[149]

According to the press, the Carter troupe, even though hampered by a lack of numbers and the illness of Carter, Mrs. Lipsis and others, performed well. Carrie Carter in *Lucretia Borgia* "sustained her reputation as a first class tragedienne" with "easy, graceful and natural" acting "devoid of coarseness and ranting."[150] In the same play Carter, demonstrating the scarcity of actors in the company, appeared in three different parts "which he rendered in an excellent manner."[151] The *Statesman* found that Miss Carter's portrayal of "Camille" ranked with the best on stage "perhaps never to be equaled in Idaho."[152]

1870 ended with a theatrical stock company residing in Boise. In late November Bartholemew, the circus man who had performed in Boise three years before, began "fitting up" Slocum's Hall at Sixth and Main as an amphitheatre for winter productions. The November 24 edition of the *Statesman* described Bartholemew's plans: "A theatrical stage will be erected with appropriate scenery, which can be moved back as occasion demands, revealing the miniature circus arena. He will have a blending of horse opera with the legitimate drama in a short time, which will be something new to Idaho."[153] The same edition revealed that Bartholemew had "sent down for a number of first class theatrical performers" that "will run quite a rivalry to the legislature catering to the public of Boise City."[154]

Bartholemew's Theatre opened on December 13 with the popular temperance melodrama, *Ten Nights in a Barroom*, as the main attraction. Admission of a dollar entitled patrons to see the play plus "educated animals, and a pantomime, interspersed with plenty of singing and dancing."[155] Bartholemew may have sent down for a company of performers, but evidently his call went unheeded. Those "artists" whose names appeared in reviews and advertising had a rather familiar, very local ring. Most were from Judge Gillespie's amateur troupe that had played as recently as November. Judge Gillespie, Graham, Minnie Chapman and Clara Lewis from the local scene joined with a dancer, Jimmy Riley, and an animal trainer, Edwards, to form the Bartholemew company. The company earned a left-handed compliment from the press for its opening night efforts when the *Statesman* noted that the play was "acted in better style than we expected."[156] The paper described the audience in a flattering manner, noting "the house was packed to repletion with the beauty and fashion of our fair metropolis."[157]

Bartholemew repeated the same bill on December 17, gave some sort of performance on Christmas Eve and offered *The Dumb Belle* on December 28. The 1870 season closed on New Year's Eve with a triple bill: *Irishmen in Petticoats*, *Rough Diamond* and scenes from a famous nautical melodrama, *Black-Eyed Susan*.[158]

1871

In 1871 the number of entertainments available to Boise residents continued to increase reaching thirty-seven documented playing days. The Bartholemew troupe supplied most of the town's entertainment, presenting a mixture of plays and variety acts through February 4 after which dramas seem to have been dropped from bills. From then to April Fools' Day Bartholemew continued to perform his tight-rope act and put Sinbad, an educated bear, through its paces. Bartholemew's name did not appear in print again until May 6 when he and the clown, Charles Graham, presented a farewell performance featuring new circus acts and "the only trained elk in the world."[159]

In addition to Bartholemew's shows Boise's population witnessed the Fort Boise Minstrels in two January presentations. The first, on New Year's Day at Fort Boise, included the talents of troupers Ward, Murphy and Evans in a burlesque titled *The Two Lovers* along with the Irish songs of Stuart, a double Irish jig by Murphy and Robbin and a drama, *Recruits Crossing the Plains*. The second show, a benefit held at Bartholemew's Theatre on January 14, raised funds for the Catholic Church that had burned a week before.[160]

The Great Western Minstrel opened a three day engagement on July 12 before a respectable audience at Good Templars Hall but the heat curtailed attendance the following two evenings. Three familiar Boise entertainers, Professor Wilkinson and the Holmans, Eugene and Kate, appeared with the minstrels. The paper, blaming the company's poor business on heat, competition and "dull times," found the group to be "worthy performers."[161]

Three touring stock companies—the Chapman Troupe, the Pixley Sisters Company and the Nathan Troupe—furnished the balance of entertainments for 1871. The Chapman Troupe, led by Carrie Chapman and Lon McCarty, came to Boise from Walla Walla, Washington on April 10 to offer a two week season. Carrie Chapman belonged to the famous Chapman family of performers who had been part of the American theatrical scene from at least the 1830's. William Chapman, founder of the acting dynasty and an early showboat manager, possibly originated the first "floating theatre" on the Mississippi. His widow sold the showboat in 1847 and the family began a slow trek westward opening up new performance territory. They reached Portland, Oregon in the summer of 1857 where various family members, such as Carrie Chapman, formed companies to tour towns in the Pacific Northwest.[162]

After three days of preparation the Chapman troupe opened on April 13 at Slocum's Hall on Front Street with the bill of *Actress of All Work* and *Artful Dodger*. The largest house of the season turned out, "with many being turned away for want of room," to witness Miss Chapman play seven characters.[163] Regular troupe members

Lon McCarty, Ellerton and Allen played in support of Miss Chapman. Evidently the troupe augmented its small numbers by recruiting the services of recognized local talent for the names of Minnie Gillespie, Charles Graham and Clara Lewis, who had acted in both Judge Gillespie's and Bartholemew's troupes, appeared in reviews of Chapman's productions. The troupe's second performance included *Caste*, a familiar Tom Robertson drama, and a play, allegedly written by Lon McCarty, entitled *How Far Is It to the Next Ranch* that was "full of happy hits at western life."[164]

Carrie Chapman's company played at Slocum's Hall through April 17 and then transferred to the Good Templars Hall because of "exorbitant charges" at Slocum's. Good Templars Hall cost less to rent and had the advantage of "being fitted up in much more comfortable style."[165] A review of the final production at Slocum's Hall on April 17 found the company's work "not up to the mark of former performances" and attributed the lapse to "distracting causes" due to the move to a new facility.[166]

The troupe reopened its season at Good Templars Hall before an excellent house on April 20 in *Retribution* and *Mr. and Mrs. Peter White*. The productions, labeled by the press as the "most successful so far," earned good notices for the local members of the company.[167] Although the troupe did good business at first in spite of what the *Statesman* termed "dull times" and lack of money, these conditions and disagreeable weather took their toll on attendance at the Chapman productions. Audiences became "slim" and Miss Chapman announced her benefit performance on April 27, a show well acted by her, but "marred by lack of support."[168] The troupe closed its Boise engagement on April 29 and departed for the Owyhees on May 1. It returned to present a poorly attended "minstrel performance" on May 13.[169] Members of the company performed in a benefit for Ellerton as late as June 6 and notice of plans for a performance in nearby

Middleton on June 10 appeared in the *Statesman*. No further mention of the Chapman troupe materialized in the paper after June 8.[170]

When the Pixley Sisters Theatrical and Variety Troupe arrived in Boise on June 16, the *Statesman* heralded the sisters' good reputation from Portland to San Francisco in its columns. Annie and Minnie Pixley (whose earlier careers have already been briefly described in the preceding chapter on Silver City) rented Good Templars Hall for their first show on June 19. The "best house of the season" greeted the opening night of *Charles II*, a performance in which Annie Pixley played the title role and Minnie portrayed "Mary Copp."[171] The press again noted the Pixley sisters' excellent recommendations and how they "fully sustained their reputations." After praising the sisters' acting the reviewer admitted, "But it was in their songs and dancing that Misses Annie and Minnie most delighted the audience."[172]

William Ellerton, Ned Campbell, Clinton and J. H. Neville all acted with the Pixley company during its first Boise engagement from June 20 to 24. Success greeted the first three performances but a production of *The Colleen Bawn* on June 24 drew negative comments from an otherwise supportive *Statesman* reviewer. He found the play well acted before an excellent house, but "beyond [the] capacity of [the] company as to numbers" and lacking in necessary stage scenery.[173] On the positive side, song and dance brought "rapturous applause and showers of boquets[sic]."[174]

The Pixley sisters' first visit proved that in Boise not all the villains were in melodramas. During their engagement letters to the editor of the *Statesman* and comments in reviews complained of J. F. Slocum and his greedy manner. Earlier, the Chapman group had changed theatres due to the high rent charged by Slocum. In addition Slocum, by some questionable practice, managed to have in his possession one of the few, perhaps the only, scenic drop curtains in town. He leveled extra charges for its use in his hall and made money by renting it out for use in other venues such as Templar Hall. Finally, he seems to have owned folding chairs which he rented to spectators at an extra fee after they had already paid the regular admission fee, usually a dollar. He did this at his own hall and could be counted on to show up at other amusement places with his chairs and cash box. Patrons could rent a chair or choose between standing or sitting on an unpadded bench during a performance. Perhaps Slocum deserved to profit from his enterprise and investment; however, he earned the resentment of press and public for practices perceived as plain avarice.[175]

On June 26 Annie and Minnie Pixley left for a tour of Idaho City and surrounding mining camps where they remained until a one-night return engagement in Boise on July 19. On this date they favored the Boise populace with *Fair Maid of Croissy* with the company "well up in their parts." The next day they departed for the Owyhee mountains. The *Statesman* reviewer could not resist making a small joke about the company's coming tour to Silver City when he wrote, "They have won golden opinions; they will now win silver opinions."[176]

When the Pixley sisters' third and last Boise theatre season began on August 3 at Good Templars Hall with a bill of *Aladdin, the Wonderful Scamp* and *Little Toodlekins*, Frank Sparrow and Clara Lewis had joined the company. Sparrow had been associated with the recently disbanded Great Western Minstrel Troupe and Miss Lewis had been a member of several local and traveling groups. After presenting *All That Glitters Is Not Gold* and *Artful Dodger* on August 5 and *Rip Van Winkle* on August 7, the sisters announced their departure for Walla Walla and Portland, a departure delayed by circumstances to August 9.[177]

The August 7 presentation of *Rip Van Winkle* also marked the benefit for William Ellerton of the Pixley company who planned to appear in the Pixley sisters' benefit on Wednesday, August 9. Ellerton celebrated his benefit by getting drunk on Tuesday "so that on the night of their [the Pixley sisters] benefit he was unfit to appear at any place but a doggery."[178] Their departure for Walla Walla postponed until August 10 by Ellerton's intemperance, the sisters incurred more expense and were further delayed by awaiting a new actor from Denver. They resumed productions at Good Templars Hall on August 12 with Tom Taylor's fine melodrama, *The Ticket-Of-Leave Man*. After several false rumors of departure, the Pixley Sisters Theatrical and Variety Troupe finally "flitted Westward to Land of the Webfooters" following its final show on August 19, a bill of *Family Jars* and *Betsy Baker*.[179] At one point in the Pixley sisters' final Boise season, the paper reported their intentions to return to play through the winter but the company never came back. Minnie Pixley, a local favorite in Portland, left the acting profession to marry in 1874. Annie, married to actor-manager Robert Fulford in 1872, later became nationally famous on Broadway in the title role of *M'liss*, then made extended tours of American in that vehicle and other popular roles.[180]

A unique theatrical company, the Nathan Juvenile Troupe (that had played in Silver City in July) entertained Boise theatre patrons in November of 1871. Made up entirely of children, the troupe featured Le Petite Marion, modestly billed as "The Eighth Wonder of the World."[181] The troupe's early notices, supplied by advance agent Vincent, emphasized its success in California and Oregon as well as in Australia.. Under the management of B. M. Nathan, the tots opened at Good Templars Hall on November 10 with presentations of *Andy Blake* and *Paddy in India*. Reviews found the acting not worthy of special mention except for Le Petit Marion who "reminds us of Lotta [Crabtree]."[182] Two boys and two other girls had "good singing and dancing capacities" but the rest were only "good average actors."[183]

Nathan's juveniles enjoyed great success during their first week in Boise but during the second week, as the press noted, the problem of the "monotony" of witnessing the same performers night after night arose. Also disputes between Nathan and the paper grew out of Nathan's failure to advertise regularly in the newspaper and not getting his poster and handbill printing done by the *Statesman*. The paper used its news columns to attack the "cheap-skate" manager. A November 21 item, alleging that Le Petite Marion had been forced to sell tickets to her benefit, ended with a message to Nathan, "Shame." On November 23, the paper accused Nathan and his "gimlet-eyed advance agent" of being "clacques" at performances by Le Petite Marion and sitting in the rear of the audience to leadoff the applause "with a great noise of clapping and stomping."[184] Although the troupe played through November 23, the paper did not print the titles of any shows after November 14. With this acrimonious situation between press and performer the eventful theatre season of 1871 came to an end.

1872

After the many amusements showered on the Boise public in 1871, the theatre season of 1872 turned out to be dreadful as only six events enlivened the entire year, four of them by a lone magician. Interest in theatre continued unabated. The *Statesman* carried news of out-of-town theatrical events such as Minnie Pixley joining George Waldron's troupe in Victoria, B.C. or her sister's marriage in Portland on April 20. In spite of interest, performance halls remained empty until Professor C. G. Stanley, "assisted by the musical talent of the city," gave a concert on May 17.[185]

Five months passed before another public performance. On November 16 magician Carl Bosco, billing himself as a "delusionist," gave a show to a standing room only crowd at Hart's Hall. His new tricks and lack of tedium in presentation earned frequent applause and the *Statesman's* praise as "a success in all particulars."[186]   After a second show on November 18 and a tour to Silver City, Bosco presented two last shows on December 4 and 5 before leaving for Salt Lake City.[187] As a final amusement for 1872 the Fort Boise "Boys in Blue," missing from theatrical circles for nearly two years, provided a welcome Christmas Day performance at their camp hall with a rather inappropriate bill of *Bombastes Furioso*, *Slasher and Crasher* and comic songs.[188]

1873

Boise theatrical offerings in 1873 increased slightly in number with local amateurs supplying half of them. With the theatrical muse once more astir at Fort Boise, the soldier-thespians continued in January where they left off in December of 1872, offering shows at the fort on January 11 and 21 under the title of the Fort Boise Dramatic Association. Reviews of the shows mention Chapman's band, the talents of Colburn and Murray, the club swinging of Jolie and the "bone and drum solo" by Coffee.[189] On January 14 the *Statesman* reviewer wrote that the "ladies of the troupe deserve special notice," adding that "Members of the legislature were quite enthusiastic over the 'Belles of the Evening.'"[190] The comments, meant to make fun of territorial legislators, referred to the common practice of soldiers playing women's roles in military entertainments. On March 7 at Good Templars Hall the Fort Boise Dramatic Association ended its productions for 1873 with a bill of *Robert Macaire* and *The Limerick Boy*. Commented the *Statesman*: "There is always a great draw when men have to assume women's characters."[191] Eugene Holman, the locally popular banjo player, also appeared and made a hit with the crowd.

Led by Chapman and Holman, local talents rendered a Grand Jubilee Concert on March 14. Performers from Fort Boise and many performers involved in previous local productions joined together in the variety show.[192] This local effort led to another on March 20 at Good Templars Hall when J. W. Houston, W. S. Anderson and Barbour, assisted by Hollister on piano, presented an evening of dramatic readings. Few showed up that night but the paper found the readings "worth seeing" and would advise repeating "if times weren't so hard ."[193]   The   Fort   Boise   Dramatic Association rewarded Eugene Holman's participation in its earlier show by holding a benefit for him at Fort Boise on March 28. The letter offering the benefit lists Michael Sullivan as president, E. W. Colburn as stage manager and J. J. Corette as secretary.[194]

Finally, in late May of 1873, professional theatre productions returned to Boise with the arrival of the veteran George B. Waldron and his troupe from their recent engagement in Baker, Oregon. Waldron brought his wife, G. W. Crosbie, S. T. Dennis, Vinson and others with him to play an initial season of five nights that began at Hart's Hall on May 28. Between June 4 and 16, the troupe went to the Idaho City area, returning to play a single show on June 17 before leaving for Silver City.[195]

A "large and appreciative audience at Good Templars Hall" on November 25 greeted Professor C. B. Plummer, a widely traveled elocutionist of some renown who had last visited Boise in 1870.[196] His rendering of "[The] Harp of a Thousand Strings" drew particular praise in a newspaper item on the event which stated that the town had been without a performance of genuine merit for some time. The same item disclosed a major dilemma affecting all theatre in the region's first decade of development. It stated: "Isolated as we are, as a general rule, no one but catch penny performers come to visit."[197] The author did not mean this general observation to apply to the elocutionist and added that Plummer possessed real talent. Plummer journeyed to Placerville and Idaho City after his Boise performance and returned on December 10 to give a second recital at Templar

Hall. Completing his Idaho engagement with a date in Silver City, he returned to his home in San Francisco.[198]

As in several years past it fell to amateurs to end the entertainment record for 1873. At Good Templars Hall of December 30 local musicians directed by Mrs. L. Scholl performed a cantata, *New Year's Eve*. Presented to raise funds for the Methodist Episcopal Church, the cantata featured fifty costumed singers and the best musicians in town.[199]

1874

A musical event opened what there was of the 1874 amusements. The Boise Turnverein sponsored a concert on February 14 featuring the Boise Orchestra and the "Most Accomplished Lady Singers of Boise City," Miss Heed, Misses Carter, Mrs. Thompson and Miss Nellie Smith, who "performed separate pieces in admirable style."[200] The success of the concert led some in the Turnverein to ponder the building of a large hall, an idea seconded in the *Statesman* of Feb. 19 in an article which pointed out that the people felt a need for a large hall in the city and that "towns and cities of any importance have such places."[201] Such yearnings for a large hall with adequate facilities, expressed sporadically throughout the decade, indicate that existing performance sites lacked adequate space for public and performer needs.

The Rosedale troupe presented four performances at Good Templar Hall's in May and June. In the opening play of *Enoch Arden* on May 26, the leading man and leading lady, Mr. and Mrs. Fulford (the former Annie Pixley), gained the good opinion of the press that praised his "natural manner" with its avoidance of "rant" and her good acting and excellent character singing.[202] The commentator evaluated the company as "above average in their profession" and "worthy of patronage."[203] The company's renditions of *Black-Eyed Susan* and *Child of the Regiment* on May 28 drew similar praise with this additional commentary on the quality of visiting acting companies: "We had gotten out of the way of theatre-going, partly by disuse, and partly because heretofore many worthless vagabonds and bilks had inflicted themselves upon us, who had no adequate conception of their assumed profession, and but little idea of decency."[204] After presenting *Hidden Hand* of May 30 and *The Lady of Lyons* on June 1 to crowded houses, the Rosedale troupe left for Silver City.

The San Francisco Minstrels entertained on August 14, left for Idaho City and then played a return engagement at Good Templars Hall on August 23 before going to Silver City.[205] To raise money for a new organ at the Episcopal Church local talent organized a grand concert on Christmas Day at Good Templars Hall, the last event in a year of meager entertainment fare.[206]

1875

The five performances which made up the whole of the entire entertainment offerings for 1875 all occurred in August. Sallie McGinley Greeley from "a pioneer family of Idaho" brought her troupe to Boise for a four-show engagement on August 18. The opening play, *Loan of a Lover*, went well "even without scenery."[207] Miss McGinley with her "full, strong and sweet" voice sang "Silver Threads Among the Gold" and Master Bobby danced, sang and played the violin.[208] Miss May also participated. The next evening the company played *Rough Diamond* to a full house at Good Templars Hall. On August 21, the night of Miss Sallie's complimentary benefit, a local merchant caused some excitement when he had the company's receipts attached for a "beef bill" dating back to a McGinley troupe visit in 1863! After closing night on August 22, Miss Sallie left for Silver City, no doubt impressed with the financial memory of Boise merchants.[209]

The only other group to play Boise in 1875 also suffered even more embarrassment than the McGinley troupe. Morrell's Minstrels tried to get up a crowd for a show on August 24 by driving around and beating a big drum during the day and giving a scene outside the hall in the evening managing by these efforts to find "only three boys willing to look at the show, if they got passes!"[210] A performance on the following night probably met with the same indifference. As the *Statesman* warned, "It is time for these itinerant fandangos to understand that people will not patronize such cheap exhibitions as the one in question."[211] The attack concluded with "But as they do their own cooking, washing and printing, and travel in their own conveyance, perhaps they make grub."[212] Doing their own printing must have been their cardinal sin. All in all, 1875 turned out to be a disastrous year for public and performer in Boise.

1876

More disaster followed for the Boise entertainment public, when 1876 turned out to be as devoid of amusement opportunities as the year before. Not a single professional troupe ventured into the area. Not one local amateur group mounted so much as a benefit. A grand total of four amateur shows, all given in a span of one month by the visiting Silver City Dramatic Association, relieved the daily routine of Boise life. The quality of the productions performed by the Silver City troupe rescued the limited theatre season from being the worst ever in Boise's brief theatre history. In a review of the group's opening bill of *Kathleen Mavoureen* and *The Stage Struck Yankee* on March 10, the *Statesman's* correspondent wrote that the troupe presented better shows than some professional traveling companies that sometimes visited the mountain towns and concluded his comments with "they are Idaho people and represent Idaho's dramatic talent, and as such are deserving of our most liberal support."[213] Professor Butler led this contingent of Idaho talent that included Miss Ada Leigh as leading lady with Mr. and Mrs. A. Bomar and Patton in supporting roles plus Professor Giles in charge of music.[214]

After demonstrating their histrionic skills in *The Stranger* and *Slasher and Crasher* on March 11, Butler's troupe either toured the basin or went back to Silver City. They returned to entertain Boise audiences on March 31 and April 1 with productions of *Chimney Corner*, *Betsy Baker*, *The Live Woman in the Mines* and *Toodles*. The *Statesman* said, "The Silver City Dramatic Association were the recipients of brilliant ovations wherever and whenever they performed in the Basin."[215]

1877

Boise theatre-goers enjoyed a resurgence of amusements in 1877 when several professional performers and acting troupes made stops in Boise between March and November with some playing more than one engagement. Local amateurs put on only one entertainment for the year, a May Day celebration which Governor Mason Brayman and the well known Bishop Daniel Tuttle attended.[216]

John Maguire—a character actor, monologist and (according to the *Statesman*) a gentleman "in all the term implies"—performed in two widely separated engagements.[217] On March 20 at Good Templars Hall he appeared as a "monologue performer" in a bill advertised as "An Olio of Oddities."[218] The show's review hailed Maguire as a first class performer who held a capacity audience "spellbound."[219] Maguire returned to Boise from Baker City, Oregon for a longer stay in October and November. An ad for his first appearance in an evening of dramatic readings at Good Templars Hall on October 27 boasted that Maguire had been "endorsed by the late General G. A. Custer."[220] Maguire enlisted the aid of some local amateurs, rehearsed for over a week and reopened at Good Templars Hall on November 6 in an old Irish farce, *O'Callaghan on His Last Legs* followed on November 8 in an unidentified bill of plays. He closed his second and last Boise season for 1877 in yet another Irish comedy, *Barney's Courtship*, on November 10. After engaging Ada and Ed Leigh and Professor Hess, he left for a tour of Basin cities with the intention of returning to Boise, but a local diphtheria outbreak caused him to bypass Boise and go to Silver City in December.[221] John Maguire went on to become a major theatrical figure in Montana where he eventually developed his own company and established a theatrical circuit. In the 1890's his theatre troupe played Boise and cities in northern Idaho.

The Huson Variety Troupe, too, made two widely separated visits to Boise. Coming from Payette, they first performed in Boise on March 28 and 29 at Good Templars Hall. Described by the press as "the best show to visit Boise in some time," the troupe featured Miss Lizzie and Miss Neenie Huson who danced and sang "exquisitely."[222] Other entertainers were Little Willie in his "silver sand jig," and two end men Billy Sherl, "the prince of Ethiopian deliniators," and Johnny Keelar.[223] Professor Huson, described by the paper as "a musician known all over the northwest" doubled as manager and pianist for his group.[224] Following their Boise performances, the Huson Troupe planned to tour Basin cities, Silver City and Alturas County. From Silver City they returned on September 29 for a single performance. By that time performers Stover, Fitzgerald and Thomas Johnson had joined Huson's variety aggregation.[225]

The major theatrical event of the year, a two-week engagement of the John Sawtelle dramatic troupe, began with a performance of *Rip Van Winkle* at Good Templars Hall on June 20. The troupe's advance man, Charles Sutherland, had arrived a few days earlier to make arrangements for the production company. A crowded house witnessed J.A. Sawtelle as Rip, supported by seven others in a performance that won extravagant praise in the press. Newspaper items promoting the June 21 production of *Driven from*

Home called Sawtelle's troupe "a splendid success," but criticized his selection of that night's play, calling it a "tired composition."[226] Despite the paper's reservation about the play, the reviewer found it "acted with such power and pathos" by Mr. and Mrs. Sawtelle, Mrs. Belle Douglas, Mrs. Murphy and Leon.[227] Samwell, an acrobatic juggler won special notice for his skills in juggling two immense balls with his feet and hands and the ability to "turn summersets on a pocket handkerchief."[228]

Sawtelle presented the perennially popular *East Lynne* on June 22 followed by the even more familiar *Uncle Tom's Cabin* on June 23. In the latter play, Sawtelle played three different characters. On June 25 Boise theatre-goers thrilled to Sawtelle's rendition of Augustin Daly's hit melodrama, *Under the Gaslight*—a play requiring several demanding scenic and technical effects.[229] Following the evening of the Daly play, the *Statesman* declared the Sawtelle company the "best troupe that has ever visited us,"[230] which would have been more meaningful if the paper hadn't printed the identical words of praise for many, many troupes over the years.

Before the Sawtelle season ended on July 7, the troupe continued to draw good crowds with productions of *David Garrick* (June 26), *Rip Van Winkle* (repeated on June 28), *Camille* (with Mrs. Sawtelle in the title role on June 29) and *Two Orphans* (July 2-3).[231] The last production, which took several days to prepare, featured Sawtelle singing a song with many local "hits" in the lyrics. Besides the song, the play held the audience "spellbound" and touched every heart with "deepest sympathy," or so the *Statesman* said.[232] The paper did not disclose the titles of the last three performances. When Sawtelle and his actors left to tour the mountain towns after July 7, the press stated they had played almost nightly for two weeks and that "no company has had a like success here."[233] Although a letter in the *Statesman* from Quartzburg announced Sawtelle's intention to return to Boise after July 21, there is no evidence that he did so.

Sawtelle and his wife continued in the theatre business for many years appearing in many western towns, especially in Montana. They eventually established themselves in New England as a major touring stock theatre troupe.

The only other entertainment entity to appear for Boise's 1877 theatre season continued the practice of playing more than once in the same year. Actually Professor E. C. Taylor, a magician, played three different engagements. He and Professor Harmon gave "combination entertainments" at Good Templars Hall on September 5 and 6 after which they went on to towns in the Basin.[234] After a rather successful tour, they returned to play Green Meadow Hall on September 19. By September 22, Taylor, billed as "necromancer, astrologer, alchemist," appeared at Good Templars Hall for a three day stay performing "refined illusions" and assisted by the accomplished actress, Mlle. La Grand.[235] For a dollar patrons could see Taylor's mystifying escape from a locked and rope bound trunk as well as a performance of the Royal Italian Marionette Troupe. After the engagement ended, Taylor again toured to Idaho City and Placerville before returning to Boise for a third time to offer shows between October 13 and 15.[236]

1878

The 1878 season offered Boise's population barely a dozen evenings of amusement, less than half of the number of attractions offered in the previous year. Professor C.B. Plummer, the elocutionist, paid a return visit to Boise on February 13 to perform at the Methodist Episcopal Church.[237] Over two months later the second entertainment group of the year rolled into town.

The Bert Dramatic Company and Lilliputian Troupe opened on April 15 and ended its season twelve days later. The actors played nightly through April 20, then announced their departure. For some unexplained reason they stayed on for another week to give an additional three performances, a benefit on April 25 for Mrs. F. W. Bert (stage name, Henrietta Osborne), and farewell matinee and evening presentations of *Our Boarding House* on April 27. During their reign in Boise, the paper also mentioned their productions of *Under the Gaslight* and *Around the World in Eighty Days.*[238]

Commodore Nutt
NYPL: Billy Rose
Collection
TH-40967

The Lilliputian Troupe with Bert's company consisted of two "big stars," Commodore Nutt and Major Nutt. Commodore Nutt, advertised as "Barnum's Original $30,000 Nutt, Smallest Man In The World," at age thirty-two stood thirty-three inches tall and weighed an even fifty pounds.[239] Major Nutt stood "just a bit bigger."[240] "Evidently the two minute actors contributed more than novelty to Bert's theatrical troupe. According to reviews Major Nutt acted in a graceful and natural manner. Commodore Nutt drew applause and roars of laughter for his "perfect personification of the drunken *Toodles.*"[241] Bert's group seemed to be a circus and a theatre company made up of the two "little people" and Master Leo Hudson, "a skillful and daring gymnast,"[242] as one part and a standard acting contingent consisting of Mr. and Mrs. Frederick W. Bert, L. A. Imhaus, J. McConnell, Miss Ella Gardner, Edwin Bert, Harry Deares, Lou Gillham and William Gillham as the other. No matter how odd the combination, Bert's troupe, hailed by the press as the "sensation of the season," drew good houses, "gave great satisfaction" and played "fully up to their advertisement."[243]

Seven months passed before Boise audiences witnessed the last few entertainments of 1878. On December 5 a group of local juvenile amateurs called "The Merry Five" pulled in a full house at

Good Templars Hall but did not merit comment from the press which remained equally silent about the appearance of Professor Rice, a mind reader who performed at Good Templars Hall on December 19.[244] The paper did comment briefly on the efforts of Mobbly, manager of the Good Templars Hall, to provide several entertainments during the winter. He fixed up the hall and hired local talent who performed under the title of "Theatre Comique." The troupe opened on December 28 and played at least one date in the early weeks of the next year. Only the names of Chapman (in charge of music), Mrs. Hill and daughter (from Idaho City) and Nettie Moulton appeared in connection with the amusement enterprise.[245] Although they won general praise in a newspaper review, the press printed no specifics items concerning works performed or members of the acting company.

1879

The theatre season of 1879 repeated the general pattern of the previous year in that a single professional company performed most of the shows presented during the year with amateurs offering a few additional entertainments. On January 24 the Theatre Comique group at Good Templars Hall that had formed in late December of the preceding year attracted a full house for a presentation of *The Dumb Boy of Manchester*, with Idaho City's Mrs. Sue Hill and her daughter in major roles, and *Nan, The Good For Nothing*.[246] Theatre Comique then merged with the recently formed Boise Dramatic Association in an unnamed joint production on January 30 at Good Templars Hall.[247] The engagement of the Ford Combination at Good Templars Hall on February 13 failed to earn any critical or other commentary from the press.[248]

Seven months passed before any other organized entertainment became available to the Boise residents. The John Thompson Troupe of six men and two women opened a season of four evenings at Good Templars Hall on September 18. Its opening production of *On Hand* prompted the *Statesman* to label them the "best troupe in years."[249] The paper listed members of the troupe as John Thompson, Miss Dotie Nagle, Miss Mollie Thompson, John MacDonald, James D. Merton, John Nicholson and Frank Moore. The company played three more nights and closed its first Boise engagement with *Around the World* on September 23. After a successful tour of the Boise Basin in which the troupe drew large houses, it played a return engagement at Good Templars Hall. In the period from October 6 to 11 John Thompson and his colleagues performed *Rip Van Winkle, Zykes, The Showman, Pike the Shanghrein* and a repeat showing of *On Hand* before their departure.[250]

In mid-October the paper announced that the Turnverein Hall at 100 South Main was being fitted up with a nice stage and scenery for a local production of *Pinafore*. The comic opera opened on October 31 to a full house and received the usual extravagant, flattering comments of a most supportive *Statesman* reviewer.[251]

Rarely did an amateur production receive anything but the most laudatory, hyperbolic and extensive of reviews. Papers might rip up a traveling troupe (especially if it had problems with the paper about its advertising and bill printing practices), but after all, amateurs were "homefolks" who often had many relatives in the community who might not take lightly to an honest appraisal of their kinfolks' thespian talents, let alone any outright negative commentary. Business considerations, public relations and editorial discretion resulted in a predictable granting of "golden opinions" to any amateur theatrical production and to anyone taking part in them. Seldom did the skills of amateur performers not equal, or exceed, those of professionals. At least that is what appeared in print.

The theatre season of 1879 ended with performances of *Little Red Riding Hood* on December 20 and 25 at Turnverein Hall. The operetta, an amateur production for the benefit of St. Michael's Church, featured a chorus of thirty little girls.[252]

The gold rush of the 1860's furnished the impetus to attract performers to early Idaho. After that, the continued existence of communities established in the mining boom brought traveling troupes of unpredictable quality into the territory on equally sporadic occasions. Other areas of the nation served by established or expanding railroad service enjoyed quality entertainment on a regular basis as theatre managers formed "circuits" for efficient and profitable distribution of the best shows that New York, Chicago and metropolitan cities had to offer. During the 1870's railways failed to develop that would connect Boise to the nation's theatrical touring routes. This created a decade of lean years for its citizens who sought entertainment in the southwestern Idaho territory.

CHAPTER 2 NOTES

[142] *Idaho Tri-Weekly Statesman.*, February 24, 1870, p. 3; March 1, 1870,p. 3.

[143] *Ibid.*, April 7, 1870, p. 3; October 8, 1870, p. 3.

[144] *Ibid.*, June 7, 1870, p. 3; August 11, 1870, p. 2.

[145] *Ibid.*, September 3, 1870, p. 3.

[146] *Ibid.*, February 10, 1870; April 16, 1870, p. 3.

[147] *Ibid.*, October 25, 1870, p.3.

[148] *Ibid.*, November 17, 1870, p. 3; November 19, 1870, p. 3.

[149] *Ibid.*, April 9, 1870, p. 3; April 12, 1870, p. 3; April 19, 1870, p. 3; April 21, 1870, p. 3; April 23, 1870, p. 3; May 6, 1870, p. 2; May 13, 1870, p. 3.

[150] *Ibid.*, April 19, 1870, p. 3.

[151] *Ibid.*

[152] *Ibid.*, April 23, 1870, p. 3.

[153] *Ibid.*, November 24, 1870, p. 3.

[154] *Ibid.*

[155] *Ibid.*, December 13, 1870, p. 3.

[156] *Ibid.*, December 15, 1870, p. 3.

[157] *Ibid.*

[158] *Ibid.*, December 20, 1870, p. 3; December 27, 1870, p. 3; December 31, 1870, p. 3.

[159] *Ibid.*, May 4, 1871, p. 3.

[160] *Ibid.*, January 5, 1871, p. 3; January 14, 1871, p. 3.

[161] *Ibid.*, July 18, 1871, p. 3.

[162] Hartnoll, p. 122; Ernst, pp. 17-18.

[163] *Idaho Tri-Weekly Statesman*, April 15, 1871, p.3.

[164] *Ibid.*, April 18, 1871, p. 3.

[165] *Ibid.*

[166] *Ibid.*, April 20, 1871, p. 3.

[167] *Ibid.*, April 23, 1871, p. 3.

[168] *Ibid.*, April 29, 1871, p. 3.

[169] *Ibid.*, May 16, 1871, p. 3.

[170] *Ibid.*, June 6, 1871, p. 3; June 8, 1871, p. 3.

[171] *Ibid.*, June 20, 1871, p. 3.

[172] *Ibid.*

[173] *Ibid.*, June 27, 1871, p. 3.

[174] *Ibid.*

[175] *Ibid.*, June 22, 1871, p. 2.

176 *Ibid.*, July 20, 1871, p. 3.

177 *Ibid.*, August 3, 1871, p. 3; August 5, 1871, p. 3; August 8, 1871, p. 3.

178 *Ibid.*, August 12, 1871, p. 3.

179 *Ibid.*, August 22, 1871, p. 3.

180 Ernst, p. 53.

181 *Idaho Tri-Weekly Statesman*, November 9, 1871, p. 2.

182 *Ibid.*, November 14, 1871, p. 3.

183 *Ibid.*

184 *Ibid.*, November 21, 1871, p. 3; November 23, 1871, p. 2.

185 *Ibid.*, May 21, 1872, p. 3.

186 *Ibid.*, November 19, 1872, p. 3.

187 *Ibid.*, November 21, 1872, p. 3; December 5, 1872, p. 3.

188 *Ibid.*, December 24, 1872, p. 3.

189 *Ibid.*, January 7, 1873, p. 2; January 14, 1873, p. 3.

190 *Ibid.*, January 14, 1873, p. 3.

191 *Ibid.*, March 11, 1873, p. 3.

192 *Ibid.*, March 13, 1873, p. 3; March 18, 1873, p. 3.

193 *Ibid.*, March 22, 1873, p. 3.

194 *Ibid.*, March 27, 1873, p. 3.

195 *Ibid.*, May 15, 1873, p.3; May 31, 1873, p. 3; June 3, 1873, p. 3; June 19, 1873, p. 3.

196 *Ibid.*, November 27, 1873, p. 3.

197 *Ibid.*

198 *Ibid.*, November 29, 1873, p. 3; December 9, 1873, p. 3.

199 *Ibid.*, December 30, 1873, p. 3.

200 *Ibid.*, February 7, 1874, p. 2; February 27, 1874, p. 3.

201 *Ibid.*, February 19, 1874, p. 3.

202 *Ibid.*, May 28, 1874, p. 3.

203 *Ibid.*

204 *Ibid.*, May 30, 1874 p. 2.

205 *Ibid.*, August 15. 1874, p. 3; August 22, 1874, p. 3.

206 *Ibid.*, December 3, 1874, p. 3.

207 *Ibid.*, August 21, 1875, p. 3.

208 *Ibid.*

209 *Ibid.*, August 24, 1875, p. 3.

210 *Ibid.*, August 26, 1875, p. 3.

211 *Ibid.*

212 *Ibid.*

213 *Ibid.*, March 11, 1876, p. 3.

214   *Ibid.*, March 18, 1876, p. 3.

215   *Ibid.*, April 1, 1876, p. 3.

216   *Ibid.*, May 3, 1877, p. 3.

217   *Ibid.*, November 15, 1877, p. 3.

218   *Ibid.*, March 20, 1877, p. 3.

219   *Ibid.*, March 22, 1877 ,p. 3.

220   *Ibid.*, October 27, 1877, p. 2.

221   *Ibid.*, November 3, 1877, p. 3; November 8, 1877, p. 3; November 10, 1877, p. 3; November 13, 1877, p. 3; December 1, 1877, p. 3; December 4, 1877, p. 3.

222   *Ibid.*, May 31, 1877, p. 3.

223   *Ibid.*

224   *Ibid.*

225   *Ibid.*, September 29, 1877, p. 3.

226   *Ibid.*, June 21, 1877, p. 3.

227   *Ibid.*, June 23, 1877, p. 3.

228   *Ibid.*

229   *Ibid.*, June 23, 1877, p. 3; June 26, 1877, p. 3.

230   *Ibid.*, June 26, 1877, p. 3.

231   *Ibid.*, June 26, 1877, p. 3; June 28, 1877, p. 3; June 30, 1877, p. 3; July 3, 1877, p. 3.

232   July 3, 1877, p. 3.

233   *Ibid.*, July 7, 1877, p. 3.

234   *Ibid.*, September 8, 1877, p. 3.

235   *Ibid.*, September 22, 1877, p. 3.

236   *Ibid.*, October 13, 1877, p. 2.

237   *Ibid.*, February 12, 1878, p. 3.

238   *Ibid.*, April 13, 1878, p. 2; April 16, 1878, p. 3; April 18, 1878, p. 3; April 23, 1878, p. 3; April 27, 1878, p. 3.

239   *Ibid.*, April 13, 1878;, p. 2.

240   *Ibid.*, April 18, 1878, p. 3.

241   *Ibid.*

242   *Ibid.*

243   *Ibid.*, April 16, 1878, p. 3.

244   *Ibid.*, December 5, 1878, p. 3; December 17, 1878, p. 3.

245   *Ibid.*, December 26, 1878, p. 3; December 31, 1878, p. 3; January 28, 1879, p. 3.

246   *Ibid.*, January 28, 1879, p. 3.

247   *Ibid.*, January 1879, p. 3.

248   *Ibid.*, February 13, 1879, p. 3.

249   *Ibid.*, September 20, 1879, p. 3.
250   *Ibid.*, September 18, 1879, p. 3; September 20, 1879, p. 3; September 23, 1879, p. 3; October 2, 1879, p. 3; October 7, 1879, p. 3; October 9, 1879, p. 3; October 11, 1879, p. 3; October 14, 1879, p. 3.
251   *Ibid.*, October 14, 1879, p. 3; November 1, 1879, p. 3.
252   *Ibid.*, December 25, 1879, p. 2; December 30, 1879, p. 3.

CHAPTER 3

Railroads and Opera Houses

Boise, Idaho: 1880-1889

In the second half of the nineteenth century the development of a national theatrical touring industry depended on the growth of the railroads. As more and more cities became accessible by trains, more and more theatrical troupes took advantage of this relatively rapid means of transportation, thus widening the geographic range of their engagements. Theatre activity, once regional in nature, gradually became centralized in New York. Here, producers formed companies called "combinations," a theatrical "package" which combined actors, scenery, costumes and all else necessary to promote and perform a single show. Local theatre owners or managers contracted for playing dates with the combination producers. The shows went on the "road," actually the railroad, during a season that lasted from late August to May of the following year. Because of the railroad touring system theatre managers in communities with a population of a few thousand or less could book as many shows as the local market would bear, even as many as four to six different plays a week. A similar system prevailed for vaudeville, circuses and other entertainments.

Because Idaho lacked any significant railroad system linking its few major towns until 1883, the territory failed to share the abundance of various entertainments available to most Americans. Even after Boise's connecting railroads became established, it took almost ten years to build a base for regularly scheduled theatre seasons. Larger and better equipped theatres had to be built to meet the needs of touring troupes. The productions needed stage space to accommodate elaborate scenery and dressing room space for large cast companies and their wardrobes. Auditoriums had to be larger, too, in order to provide enough seating to increase the box office income sufficiently to meet the costs of touring productions and to allow profits for both the show's producer and the local theatre owner.

It also took some time to establish a community's reputation as a "show town," one that would readily support stock theatre, touring shows or other amusement forms. Even if some Idaho communities gained a good reputation for attending theatre, the long distances between towns could make managers reluctant to book them. Traveling shows preferred short "hops" between engagements, usually a hundred miles or less which was easy to achieve in the more densely populated areas of eastern and mid-western America. Certainly managers must have been less than enthused about the "long haul" between Pocatello and Boise, one of the longest in the nation. It took the ten years between 1883 and 1893 for Idaho towns, theatre owners and the public to overcome obstacles to the growth of the state's entertainment and cultural needs. Not all regions progressed at the same rate; in some instances towns became less attractive to entertainers due to adverse economic factors and a consequent loss of population. But the general direction continued upward in a decade of growth that saw a gradual increase in the number of professional touring companies coming to already established theatre stops in Idaho cities such as Boise and Lewiston and the creation of theatres in developing communities such as Pocatello and Wallace.

The long-awaited connection of Boise to a transcontinental railroad near the beginning of Boise's third decade of theatrical history did not immediately transform the entertainment scene in what was to be the capital city. For the first few years touring companies traveling by rail could only reach the vicinity of Boise. After arriving at Kuna, Idaho (southwest of Boise) they still faced over ten miles of travel by stage to reach Boise. By the late 1880's a railroad spur was built between Nampa, Idaho and Boise and replaced the stage line between Kuna and Boise, but even then rail service and scheduling often proved too undependable for touring companies, especially in winter.

1880

While the entertainment calendar of 1880 expanded to about twenty days of presentations, not a single professional theatre troupe found its way to Boise. The city attracted only three professional entertainers of any kind during the entire year. Amateur productions, civilian and military, provided the majority of what few diversions there were.

After almost seven years of military theatrical inactivity, soldiers revived the Fort Boise Minstrels for a series of appearances in 1880, the first at Good Templars Hall on January 9. After Boise amateurs presented *Pinafore* on January 17 (a very successful repeat performance of their October, 1879 production), the Fort Boise Minstrels mounted their own burlesque version of the comic opera at Good Templars Hall, first on January 29 and then on February 16.[253] The minstrels concluded their winter productions at Good Templars Hall on March 4 with G. Company's rendition of *Pocohontas*, a "well rendered" show featuring a cast of Miss Keown, Mahlon and Sexton.[254] Performances by the military men ceased until the autumn of 1880 when the minstrels appeared at Good Templars Hall on November 12, 13 and 16, the company augmented by three visiting professionals— West, Coughlin and Eddie Dwyer, a clog dancer. The minstrels continued to appear during November and December in conjunction with other professional and amateur groups.[255]

After an engagement in Umatilla, Oregon Professor C. B. Plummer paid a return visit to Boise on January 16 for a two night season at the Presbyterian Church.[256] The elocutionist planned to perform again on January 29, but for some reason only passed through town on his way to Silver City.[257]

Fourteen years after his last appearance in Boise, John Kelly returned to receive the town's welcome and regard. The fabled violinist and his wife, a fine pianist, stayed at the Overland Hotel and performed a successful concert before a "large and appreciative audience" at the Turnverein Hall on January 22.[258] Two days later they left to tour his "old stomping grounds" in the Basin, Idaho City, Placerville, Centerville and Quartzburg. Although he did not perform in Boise on February 14 when he passed through on his way to Silver City, he did return on March 10 to receive a complimentary benefit at Turnverein Hall. After his tour ended he and his wife returned to their home in Oakland, California.[259]

As in the past two years, Boise citizens experienced a gap of over six months between entertainment opportunities, from the Kelly benefit in March to the appearances of Charles A. Lewis on October 1 and 2 at Good Templars Hall. Lewis, a magician, supposedly had been in Boise four years before, although his name did not appear in the papers at that time. His company enjoyed "turn away" houses for their first two shows in Boise. Professor Frank Cassel of the troupe helped publicize the performances by walking a rope stretched across the street from Good Templars Hall. Other entertainments given outside the theatre before curtain time also helped to promote the magic show. Following his tour of the Boise Basin towns, Lewis brought his company back to Boise for two final performances on October 18 and 19.[260]

Odds and ends of entertainments concluded the 1880 season. The Amateur Dramatic Society of Boise rendered *Among the Breakers* to a capacity crowd at Good Templars Hall on October 30.[261] As mentioned above, the Fort Boise Minstrels played three nights in November. In the period between November 20 and 25 a group named the "Capital Varieties" charged a quarter for its performances at Earley's Theatre. Described as a "sort of go-easy minstrel variety show," the troupe featured the talents of Miss Grace Dashwood.[262] It is not clear whether Earley's Theatre was an actual location or, as sometimes happened, the manager's name attached to an existing building such as Templar Hall. The Fort Boise Minstrels and the Boise City Combination Troupe jointly held a benefit show on Christmas Day, the final performance of 1880.[263]

One other company may have provided shows for the Boise public during 1880, the Troubador Comedy Company. No mention of this group appeared in the columns of the *Statesman* during the period between September and December, but on January 1, 1881 the paper reported the troupe's plans to tour the Basin and described it as a group of local talents that had played Boise "in autumn and winter."[264] The *Statesman* reported nothing further about the group.

1881

If 1880 had been generally uneventful in terms of available opportunities to attend entertainments, 1881 turned out to be nearly eventless with only seven shows for the entire year and only one of them by a so-called professional group. About April 21 the Hill-Moulton theatrical troupe left Boise to play Wood River and Bellevue after playing in Boise since April 15. B. F. Moore managed the troupe with D. Boone as music director. Sketchy newspaper items indicate the troupe played the Basin as well as Boise. The names Hill and Moulton, familiar in Boise and Idaho City, suggest that the troupe was of local origin and more amateur in nature than truly professional.[265]

Boise amateurs and the Fort Boise Minstrels presented a handful of shows in a period of four months in a theatrical season that ended on April 22. Eight months would pass before any further entertainers would tread the Boise boards. The minstrels gave an entertainment on January 22 at Good Templars Hall. They played again on April 4 at the same site.[266]   The Boise City amateurs presented an opera, *The Doctor of Alcantra*, at Turnverein Hall on February 26 and repeated it on March 1.   The same group again presented *Pinafore*, the local hit of the 1880 season, on April 22 at Turnverein Hall as a benefit for Mr. and Mrs. H. Z. Burkhart who had directed shows for the amateurs.[267]

1882

The dearth of professional entertainment in Boise ended in 1882 when five theatrical troupes came to town, swelling the number of shows almost tenfold to a total of over forty.   Fort Boise soldiers presented the only amateur productions.   They opened the theatrical season with variety entertainments on January 6 and February 3 at Good Templars Hall under the name of the Boise Barracks Variety Troupe and closed the year as the Fort Boise Minstrels with a show at the post on December 22 and one at Good Templars Hall on December 26.[268] In between these military amusements, professional companies contributed to the entertainment bill in Boise when several stopped by on their way to try their luck in the Wood River mining boom at Hailey, Idaho.

The parade of professional entertainers began May 6 at Good Templars Hall with an appearance of Professor Schumann, advertised modestly as "The World's Greatest Magician."[269]   Next, on May 27 at the same site, the William J. Tennant Company offered a single performance of T. E. Wilkes' comedy, *The Miser*. Tennant's troupe returned on June 23 to present *Christmas Eve*. Both plays earned a fine reception with the company receiving compliments for "being well up in their parts."[270]   Members of the troupe included Mr. and Mrs. Tennant, James Anderson, Henley, Hire, Colbert, Brophy and Miss Lyle.[271]   In between the Tennant Company engagements, Professor Barley and Williams performed a "magical" concert on June 6 at Good Templars Hall with Barley playing the violin and Williams singing to the accompaniment of his guitar.[272]

The Nellie Boyd Company performed the longest theatrical engagement of 1882 with a season extending from August 10 through the 19th at Good Templars Hall. The company's notices emphasized its new scenery, full brass band and full orchestra. Admission cost $1.25 with a seven performance ticket available for $6.25. Anticipating the summer heat in Boise, company publicity stressed that the hall would be cooled as much as possible and that ice water would be dispensed between acts. *Fanchon, the Cricket* opened the season followed by *A Case for Divorce* on August 11, *Kathleen Mavourneen* for the August 12 matinee and *A Celebrated Case* for the evening show. After resting on Sunday, the troupe continued to present plays from its impressive repertory of standard and popular dramas beginning with *East Lynne* on August 14, *Forget Me Not* the next day and *The Two Orphans* on August 16. Nellie Boyd played the title role in *Camille* on August 17 before a crowded house. The company ended their season with *The Octoroon* on Friday, August 18 and two Saturday shows, a matinee performance of *The Millionaire's Daughter* and a final evening presentation of *The New Magdalen*. When Miss Boyd and her troupe left for Hailey and Bellevue, Idaho, the press expressed regrets over their departure.[273]

Only two days passed before another dramatic company rang up the curtain at Good Templars Hall. On August 22 Boise theatre patrons welcomed a troupe with a familiar name from the city's theatrical past, the McGinley Comedy Company, that had not

Nellie Boyd
Harvard University
Houghton Library
Meserve Collection

appeared in town since 1875. The McGinley group only offered one show, *The Golden Cross*, before heading to Idaho City where members of the McGinley clan some twenty years before had played a part in the establishment of theatre in Idaho. Their show, "a military drama" presented with "new scenery, new and elegant wardrobe, brass band and orchestra," won a favorable but tepid review.[274]

The Novelty Combination Company entertained Boise audiences during two engagements, a very short one on September 4 as the troupe passed through on the way to Silver City and a substantial one of over two weeks beginning on September 20 at Good Templars Hall.[275] The paper called the troupe's first performance "the best variety appearance in years." During the second and longer season, the performers attracted large and well pleased audiences. The *Statesman* noted that, while only six people made up the combination, those six could "crowd more into two hours than any other group seen in Boise."[276] Of the six only the names of Downs and Allicoat appeared in print with Allicoat winning recognition for his jig dancing. The troupe then left Boise on October 8 with an announced itinerary of Middleton, Emmettsville, Weiser, Baker, Portland and San Francisco.[277]

The Frank Cleaves Dramatic Combination became the last theatrical company to play Boise in 1882 when it opened at Good Templars Hall on November 20 with a Cleaves' specialty, *Shingwan, the Outlaw of '98*. Following a Sunday hiatus Cleaves reopened with *The Child of the Regiment* followed on Tuesday night with *Enoch Arden*. The season ended on November 24 and 25 with productions of *Black-Eyed Susan* and *Lost in London*. Performances met with standing-room-only audiences and the press expressed the hope that Cleaves and his actors would return. Return they did on December 5 and 6 with a rendition of *The French Spy*. For their return engagement they added the old local favorite, John B. Robinson, who had not appeared in Boise for the last sixteen years, to the company.

Notices listed only one other performer during the troupe's engagements, Emma Heath Cleaves.[278]

Except for the final presentations of the Fort Boise Minstrels, the 1882 theatre season ended with the departure of the Cleaves Combination. J. B. Robinson remained behind to establish a theatre of his own in Boise. The *Statesman* of December 14 reported that he leased the Pavilion on the Capital block with plans to remodel the thirty-four by eighty foot structure into a theatre and dance hall with a twenty-four by thirty-four foot stage. By the nineteenth he advertised that a Grand Opening Ball would be held on December 25 at Robinson's Dancing Academy in the "New Opera House."[279] Robinson's Opera House would be the site of many entertainments in the years to follow.

1883

In September of 1883, as the second decade of Idaho theatre history neared its end, workers for the Oregon Short Line Railroad completed the route as far as Kuna, over ten miles from Boise. Boiseans had access to the railroad station by means of a twice-a-day stage service between Kuna and Boise. This long awaited event naturally had a great impact on all aspects of life in Boise and would eventually have far reaching consequences for the city's cultural activities. However, Boise's connection to a transcontinental rail system did not transform the entertainment scene immediately. It would take several years to establish touring routes with booking agents and for larger local theatres to be built to meet the economic and production demands of professional touring combinations.

Despite the arrival of the Oregon Short Line, little changed on the local entertainment scene during 1883. Boise's theatre public had access to over thirty evenings of amusement with about one-third of the theatrical activity supplied by local amateur organizations.

Most of the professional entertainment occurred in the last half of the year.

The season began on January 19 at Good Templars Hall with a production of *Ten Nights in a Barroom* by a local amateur group, the Red Cross Dramatic Club, which repeated the temperance melodrama and a comedy, *More Blunders*, on January 30. Professor R. F. Beale and Pomeroy, leaders of the group, made "sundry improvements" of Good Templars Hall including new scenery painted by Beale.[280] Beale, who had a marble and stone-cutting business, reportedly had some previous professional theatre experience. His name appeared often in connection with amateur theatre in Boise and later with theatres in northern Idaho.

Also on January 30, John Robinson and his Home Amateur Dramatic Company presented the farcical *Sleeping Car* at Robinson's "New" Opera House. The paper reported no further shows at Robinson's until February 24 when John and William Robinson along with "numerous volunteers" joined vocalist Emma Lawrence in a vocal and dramatic concert that drew a full house. Illness delayed Miss Lawrence's next performance until March 17 at which time she and the Robinsons presented a bill that included John Robinson's rendition of Hamlet's soliloquy, *Why Don't She Marry?* (a musical burletta), and a hornpipe dance by William Robinson. All were reviewed favorably, especially John Robinson in the "To Be Or Not To Be" soliloquy. Robinson offered *The Irish Heiress* on March 22 with La Petite Laura, a young Robinson child said to have been born in Boise City. Productions of *Kathleen Mavourneen* and *That Rascal Pat* followed on March 31. Robinson repeated the former play along with *Barney the Baron* for a benefit given to honor R. F. Beale and a Miss Danforth on April 4.[281]

No further report of shows at Robinson's appeared in the *Statesman* until June 6 when Miss Emma Lawrence took a benefit in the play *Dora*. On June 6 La Petite Laura also took a benefit, selecting a rather shopworn comedy, *Naval Engagements*, for her vehicle. After this the Robinson family seems to have departed from Boise.[282]

A group with the colorful name, Leo's Ideal Pleasure Party, began a four-night stand at the opera house on June 20. The Leo Brothers drew well and gave satisfaction with a variety entertainment of songs, dances, recitations, farces, acrobatic feats and a trapeze act. After a tour of the Basin, the Leo Brothers returned for another engagement on June 30. They played to crowded houses every night until they closed on July 7.[283] They may have gone to the Wood River mining camps before once again returning to Boise as the Leo Brothers Circus. Ads for the two daily shows on September 8 and 10, admitted that there would be no big street parades, no hundreds of chariots, but that the Leo Brothers Circus would present "A Galaxy of Professional Stars."[284] At any rate, they charged a professional one dollar for admission. The circus, about the first to ever come to Boise since Bartholomew's earlier shows in 1867 and the 1870's, left for Payette and Weiser, Idaho after its Boise season.[285]

Between engagements by the Leo Brothers, the Greeley Comedy Company played at the opera house on August 30 to only a fair audience. Sallie McGinley Greeley formerly of the McGinley company that played Boise a year earlier, acted in a major role.[286]

Coincident with the opening of rail access to Boise, the *Statesman* on September 20 printed a story about R. F. Beale accepting the "position of Circuit Agent for all the theatrical companies that will leave San Francisco this winter for Portland, Ore."[287] According to the article, Beale would make all arrangements and appointments for companies to visit Boise by way of Walla Walla, Washington and that he was well suited for the position. Although the item said the Alice Harrison troupe would arrive in the middle of October and that other attractions would follows at "short intervals," plans did not pan out. Although the quality and quantity of shows playing at Boise increased after the establishment of the rail connection, it took another ten years before companies followed each other at short intervals through any part of Idaho. October editions of the paper reported Beale, "the theatrical circuit agent," as devoting his leisure time to painting a drop curtain for the opera house.[288] He may have also painted an advertising curtain featuring a scene on the Rhine for the same facility. As part of his preparation for hosting touring shows, Beale engaged E. Green, an Idaho artist, to paint an entirely new set of scenery for the opera house.[289]

Paul Boulon, leader of a musical troupe which performed on October 12 and 13, claimed to be returning after an absence of eight years and that he had "played night after night" years ago in Boise. He may well have, but the earlier papers failed to mention his presence or performance. His skill as a violinist and his Ladies' Cornet Band made a hit before full houses. After a tour of the Basin, Boulon and company again played Boise on October 19 at Good Templars Hall.[290] A week later, on October 26, at the same hall the Fort Boise Minstrels made their only appearance for the year.[291]

The quite popular Katie Putnam Company played the final engagement of the 1883 season. Katie Putnam had earned a good reputation in western theatre and played in that arena for many years. She would return to Boise and other Idaho cities several times in years to come. Her engagement appears to be the first one arranged and contracted for by R. F. Beale. The full engagement turned out to be most successful, but the press failed to list any plays or specific playing dates. The company arrived on November 24, played to good houses, gave "excellent satisfaction,"

Katie Putnam
NYPL: Billy Rose
Collection
TH-45064

and closed on December 1.[292] Sometime in this period the company presented *The Old Curiosity Shop*, a play closely associated with Katie Putnam throughout her career.

1884

In spite of the mixed blessings of the new railroad, only two professional theatrical companies visited Boise to play extended seasons in 1884. Two magicians, a circus and a musical concert added to the professional calendar of amusements. Four amateur events completed the relatively abundant season of over thirty events.

George Holland, supported by Miss Constance Murielle and the Holland Comedy Company performed at Good Templars Hall from January 25 to February 2 of 1884. While in Butte, Montana on January 10, Holland had advertised his intentions to come to Boise with Nellie Boyd, who had played the town earlier, in his company. However, Miss Boyd's name did not appear in newspaper items when the company played Boise but the names of Buckingham, Calhoun, Deal, Murphy, Murray, Miss Douglass, Miss Johnston, Miss Aiken along with Holland and Miss Murielle did.[293]

Holland, noted for his portrayal of Lord Dundreary in *Our American Cousin* led off his Boise season with that popular comedy and attracted an "overcrowded and fashionable" audience of Boise's best citizens.[294] On the next seven nights he produced a rather standard repertory of comedies and melodramas including *Led Astray* and *The Ticket-*

George Holland
University of Washington
Libraries Special Collections
PH Coll 75.305

Of-Leave Man. The press awarded rave reviews to the troupe labeling it the best to ever play Boise (a description applied too often over the years to too many troupes to be meaningful). Holland himself received special notice for his ability to play serious as well as comic roles. After a most successful season, Holland and company departed for Salt Lake City on February 3.[295]

On July 28 the Phosa McAllister Company became just the second professional stock touring troupe to play Boise in 1884. Billed at the "Boise Opera House" (a new name for Good Templars Hall) for four nights, the company actually remained for seven nights and did not leave until August 7. They had performed in Hailey as late as July 22 and came to Boise at the insistence of John Maguire, the same actor who had played Boise in 1877.[296] He now controlled principal theatres in Oregon, Washington and Montana territories and acted as general manager for several companies. During the McAllister engagement the press reported Maguire would visit Boise with the possibility of building a theatre, a "pressing need" in the community.[297] The "possibility" never materialized.

Phosa McAllister's opening performance of *Ingomar, the Barbarian* on July 28 elicited a fine *Statesman* commentary. The "largest audience ever assembled here on a similar occasion" rewarded the cast with an "appreciative and enthusiastic reception."[298] With a planned performance of *Frou Frou* cancelled due to misplaced scenery (one of the hazards of touring), the company substituted *Romance of a Poor Young Man* for its second production. The paper found it no less than a "triumph" with special accolades for

Phosa McAllister
University of Washington
Libraries Special Collections
UW12345

Miss McAllister and her unrivalled "personations." The review also mentioned Fox, Miss Lathrop, Miss Josephine, Lewis, Fitzgerald and Miss Gracie. Fox drew special notice as an actor who had played Boise eighteen years before in support of Julia Dean Hayne during the town's earliest theatre seasons.[299]

The McAllister Company acted *Leah, the Foresaken* on July 30 and with the finding of the "misplaced" *Frou Frou* scenery presented that play the following night. *Ruby Cross* and the ubiquitous *Uncle Tom's Cabin* entertained audiences during the first two nights of August. On August 4 a "slightly diminished audience" greeted Phosa McAllister in the title role of *Camille* as Boiseans headed for the cooler climes of the mountains.[300] A benefit performance of *The Lady of Lyons* for the Ladies' Aid Society on August 6 delayed the departure of the McAllister Company for Weiser, Idaho.

Some five or six weeks later Phosa McAllister's troupe returned from engagements west of Boise and played four nights beginning September 18. Productions of *Cynthia, Rosedale, Fanchon* and *Engaged* made up a brief season that drew good houses in spite of a second appearance by the company in so short a time. Again the *Statesman* described the entire company as "far better than any that has ever visited our city."[301] Phosa McAllister merited favorable and flattering comparison with several contemporary actresses.[302] The *Statesman* editor invited the company to return after it left for Hailey and other sites in Idaho's Wood River region.

As for other touring entertainments, two concerts by the nationally renowned Nashville Students (a minstrel group) equaled or surpassed the success of the two dramatic companies in attracting Boise audiences. On June 21 the *Statesman* wrote that 150 tickets had been sold at Pinney's bookstore in just two hours. By the time the "Students" arrived on June 28 few seats remained but the local sponsor quickly and successfully negotiated for a second concert. As the paper observed, "Boise City audiences are never easily pleased," but delighted in the "Students."[303]

Two magicians amazed and entertained Boise patrons with their trickery in 1884. Signoir Martel, a mute magician, booked the Casino Saloon for a three day engagement on July 3 and then appeared at Good Templars Hall on July 9 before going on to Caldwell.[304] That "Delineator of Black Art," Anton Zamlock, occupied the Boise Opera House for four nights beginning August 18.[305] Neither wizard elicited more than minimal press commentary.

J. B. Shaw's Silver Plate Circus rolled into Boise on July 3 for a three day stay that added to the usual July 4 festivities in Boise. The only circus of the summer presented shows twice a day and claimed to be the "The Biggest, The Grandest, The Fairest [and] The Squarest."[306] Advertising urged citizens to "Read all the bills, Have your houses in readiness, Tell the old folks, Tell the children, Tell everybody."[307]

Four amateur productions filled intervals between professional engagements in 1884. Under the direction of R. F. Beale an amateur group packed Good Templars Hall on February 25 with a bill of *Shingawn* and a comic operetta, *Il Jacobi*, to raise funds for the Boise Library.[308] On March 17 at Good Templars Hall amateurs produced *The Last Loaf* with Mr. Beale in the leading role.[309] *The Pirates of Penzance*, "long in preparation" by local amateurs, delighted capacity audiences on April 16 and 19 when presented as a benefit for the City School Library fund.[310] A production of *Black-Eyed Susan* and *Larry the Blunderer* by the Boise Amateur Drama Club closed out the theatrical year on December 9 at Good Templars Hall. Mr. and Mrs. Richard Beale and Major N. H. Camp starred in this benefit performance for the local band which turned out to be, according to the press, an artistic and financial success.[311]

1885

In 1885 Boise experienced a slight drop in the number of amusements presented, slightly over twenty being offered for the year. Amateur efforts held the stage until February, then a mixture of theatre troupes, magic shows, minstrels, circuses and concerts followed at intervals during the remainder of the year.

The Boise City Amateur Dramatic Society promoted its January 20 and 22 productions of *The Streets of New York* by emphasizing its efforts in the remodeling of Good Templars Hall for a big railroad scene, a scene added to Boucicault's famous melodrama just for the present production. Richard Beale as Badger won the acclaim of the large audience as well as that of the *Statesman* reviewer who gave generous praise to the entire cast. However, he did find fault with an   accident in the presentation of the much publicized railroad scene.[312] On February 7 at Good Templars Hall members of the Boise City Brass Band rewarded R. F. Beale for his work on their behalf and for his contributions in general to amateur theatre by rendering him a benefit performance of *Robert Emmett* and *Handy Andy*.[313]

Professional entertainments in 1885 began when the Whelan Dramatic and Musical Alliance Company opened for three days at Good Templars Hall on February 9. A "large and appreciative audience" applauded the initial show, *Uncle Josh Whitcomb*, and the acting of its cast: M. M. Whelan, M. S. Wilson, Mac M. Barnes, W. A. Campbell, Frank A. Rogers, Miss Sadie Stringhorn, Miss Belle Castleton, Miss Irene Forest and Master Russell. Whelan's troupe offered *The Hidden Hand* on February 10 and closed the brief season the next night with a double bill of *The Farmer's Iron Will* and *The Fool of the Family*.[314]

About February 17 the advance man for the Katie Putnam Company with the intriguing name of "Alphabet" Williams, arrived in town to begin promoting Miss Putnam's Boise season, set to commence on March 9. Miss Putnam, headed east on the Oregon Short Line Railroad, would play in Boise for six nights. The paper hailed Miss Putnam as "Boise City's favorite" on her opening night in *Lena, the Madcap*. Following her appearance on March 10 in one of her specialties, *The Old Curiosity Shop*, a reviewer noted her ability to play both comic and serious roles. He added that Katie Putnam "is an excellent little actress, quick, vivacious, has a clear musical voice, sings and dances well and possesses great powers of mimicry. Her versatility of talent is wonderful."[315] Her success in attracting large crowds led the *Statesman* to print yet another article on the need for a new opera house which expressed the hope that the next man who built a brick building on Main Street would add a second story opera house and hall.

Between March 11 and 14 the Putnam troupe presented *The Little Detective, The Pearl of Savoy, Little Sunflower* and *Meg, the Farmer's Daughter*. Besides Miss Putnam only the names of Miss Carrie Radcliffe and James A. Devlin appeared in connection with productions. Houses remained filled to witness Miss Putnam "as her friends are many and her enemies none." After leaving Boise the troupe opened in Hailey, Idaho on March 16.[316]

When Signor Bosco, magician, played the Boise Opera House between April 8 and 10, his advertising listed R. F. Beale and Joe Simons as manager and agent for the opera house. Several days later J. W. Baird's Mammoth Minstrel Troupe booked the hall for April 21 and 22. R. F. Beale received credit for making arrangements that included raising seats at the back of the hall to afford a better view.[317]

The next professional production, Dan Morris Sullivan's *Grand Tour of Europe* and *Original Mirror of Ireland* on May 13 and 14, promised "panoramic views, playing and personifications."[318] This show with its cast of ten elicited no direct response from the press; however a related item that alluded to work beginning immediately on the capital building concluded, "It is probable that the panoramic performance will be the last one at the opera house on its present site."[319]

June and July turned out to be notable for dramatic companies that did not come to town. Miss Laura Dainty, booked for mid-June, evidently chose not to perform in Boise after all. When the paper printed a rumor that the world famous Madame Janauschek and her company would perform July 7 to 10 at Good Templars Hall, the editor remarked that the public was "hardly willing to believe that she would come to Boise City."[320] The *Statesman's* skepticism was well founded. Although Janauschek did act in Boise in later years, she was a "no show" in July of 1885.

To the delight of children of all ages, J. B. Cushing's Great Overland Circus set up tents in Boise on July 16. The aggregation proudly boasted "We have an Old Time Circus Of Our Boyhood Day," which probably meant it was a small circus.[321] Only the barest of comment appeared in the press concerning the return of the Nashville Students in concert at Good Templars Hall on August 25.[322]

A full house attended the final performance at Good Templars Hall on November 30 when the Alvin Joslin Comedy Company attempted to make good on its promise of "180 laughs in 180 minutes."[323] The troupe also advertised an "Operatic Solo Orchestra" and a "$10,000 Challenge Band."[324] The company manager responded to complaints about the dollar and a half admission charge by stating that it took $300 per day to run the troupe. This did not include the stage fare from Kuna to Boise for the twenty people in the company and freight charges for a special small set of scenery.[325]

As early as mid-September, while preparations for closing Good Templars Hall were under way, James B. Taylor and Henry Hammond planned to convert an existing skating rink into a multiple use hall suitable for theatrical purposes as well as dancing and skating.

The structure, located at Main and Tenth Streets, had ground floor dimensions of thirty-six feet wide by eighty feet long and a height of nineteen feet. Plans called for the building of a stage twenty feet square and the addition of dressing rooms in a ten by twenty foot area. The estimated seating capacity was 500 for this new facility, named Capital Hall.[326]

1886

The Boise theatre season of 1886 resembled the lean seasons of the previous decade as only a handful of companies offered a total of less than a dozen entertainments. The *Statesman* printed nothing in the way of local amusement items until late August. The change from Templar Hall to Capital Hall as the city's theatre facility in the middle of the theatrical year may have prevented the new theatre managers from securing bookings until the next season. Whatever the reason, Boiseans went without even amateur theatricals for ten months.

Finally, on September 16 the Boise entertainment season began with the arrival of W. W. Cole's New Colossal Shows, a circus with fifty actors and specialists offering thirty minutes of theatre and thirty minutes of Wild West. Cole's show played Weiser and Caldwell, Idaho the two days before setting up in Boise and then went on to Shoshone and Hailey, Idaho.[327] Cole's must have been a railway operation since there were no gaps between playing days.

The Golden Bell Comedy Company had the honor to be the first acting company of record to play in Boise's Capital Hall. They opened for three nights on October 20 promising a change of program each night, programs not printed in the paper, unfortunately. Fair audiences enjoyed the troupe's "chaste entertainment," offerings of minstrelsy, comedy and burlesque.[328]

Almost two months later, on December 20, the J. G. Stuttz New York Theatrical Company of twenty-two people began a week's run at Capital Hall. The first show, *A Celebrated Case*, won the good opinion of the press that singled out Mr. Stuttz, Miss Alma Stuttz and Little Iva as particularly talented. Stuttz performed a rather standard repertoire of dramas including *The Pearl of Savoy*, *Lucretia Borgia* and *Lady Audley's Secret*. A performance of the usually surefire *East Lynne* on December 23 attracted only a small house due to competition, a speech by Governor Stevenson. Although the paper quit listing the titles of Stuttz's productions after December 25, the troupe continued to perform in and around Boise during the last week of 1886.[329]

1887

The Stuttz New York Theatrical Company began the 1887 theatre season on New Year's Day with farewell matinee and evening performances before departing to play Weiser on January 4. The *Statesman* gave a glimpse of performance conditions when it wrote this opinion of Stuttz and his company. "It would be a great pleasure to see Mr. and Mrs. Stuttz . . . when the scenic setting was in strict accord with the play, and , even as it is, playing with no especial accessories, and but fair support, they have . . . drawn fair houses every night."[330]

The final shows by the Stuttz company which opened the 1887 season represented the first of some twenty performances given in the year, most of them by professional groups. Unfortunately the press saw fit to print only the barest of information about troupes and their shows and often omitted play titles and the names of any but star performers.

Katie Putnam and her company paid a return visit to Boise on January 13, opening in *Erma the Elf*—a play especially suited to her talents. She played two more nights before leaving for Hailey.[331] Little over a month later, on February 19 and 21, local talent produced the oratorio, *Queen Esther*, at Capital Hall.[332] Another month passed and then, on March 29 and 30, Boiseans witnessed *Uncle Tom's Cabin*, not just the old, familiar, ordinary show, but McFadden's Boston Double Uncle Tom's Cabin Company with special scenery and two of everything—two Uncle Toms, Two Little Evas, two Topsies, etc.[333] McFadden's version of the play followed production trends of the day by embellishing the old popular work with variety and specialty acts of all descriptions.

The Nellie Boyd Company, which had played Boise some three years before, returned on April 25 for a week's engagement. Boyd's company utilized the larger stage of Capital Hall for presentation of its scenic effects, the press alluding to "remarkable mechanical effects" in the opening play, *Unknown*.[334] *Passion's Slave*, the following production, featured one scene with a "ship moving at full speed.[335] Although not reported in the paper, three other plays produced during the troupe's stay—*Lost in London, The Octoroon* and *The Streets of New York*—all had one or more spectacular scenic effects such as a Mississippi steamboat or a burning tenement house.

Single evening events or short term engagements made up the remainder of the 1887 season. All shows except a circus played at Capital Hall. On June 6 a traveling company presented the popular comedy of *Peck's Bad Boy*.[336] J. W. Baird's Mammoth Minstrels occupied the hall on June 28 and 29.[337] The Pattie Sisters gave a program of readings, impersonations and musical monologues on August 2.[338] On August 30 Madame F. Roena Medini (born Frankie Miller in Idaho City) returned to Boise and appeared with local talent in a concert.[339] She had studied opera in Italy and acquired the more exotic name of Medini. S. H. Barrett's New United Monster Show performed under canvas on September 25 as the last attraction of the year.[340]

1888

Two important things occurred in the theatrical year of 1888, one positive and one negative. In October Peter Sonna revealed that the upper floor of his brick building, referred to as his "new brick" or "Sonna's brick," would be made into an opera house. The *Statesman* reported that "The stage will be large and supplied with the latest improvements" including all new scenery and a roomy gallery.[341] A November newspaper item disclosed that "seats of the latest pattern had

Peter Sonna
Idaho State
Historical
Society 408-A

been ordered" to fill the 700 to 800 seat capacity of the new auditorium.[342] Although not dedicated nor used until early in 1889, the planning and building of the Sonna Opera House proved to be the most positive news for Boise theatre patrons in 1888.

On the negative side, shortly before July 8 the Boise City Council raised the fee for theatrical licenses from three to ten dollars. Capital Hall managers Hammond and Taylor objected and an anonymous writer sent a letter to the *Statesman* in protest against the fee raise. In part the letter pointed out that Boise "must depend on traveling companies . . . and they come at heavy expense and seldom make any money, barely enough to make expenses."[343] The writer argued that the old license was all the market would bear and that higher fees "must be construed as unfriendly legislation against theatre and opera houses."[344] In spite of objections, the fee increase stood. From time to time further objections to the theatre license rate appeared in the paper. In September an item contained a plea to the council to reduce the rate to five dollars when Mr. Taylor of Capital Hall reportedly had to send away an opera company because of the ten dollar license. Even in the news items about Sonna's Opera House the paper still objected to the "high" license fee.[345]

The license fee and other factors reduced the theatre season of 1888 to slightly fewer than twenty performances rather evenly divided between amateur and professional groups. Capital Hall housed all entertainments save one minstrel show at the Boise Barracks on August 7.

Amateur theatricals opened and closed the theatrical season with the Dramatic Club opening the year on January 12 with a double bill of *Loan of a Lover* and *Enlisted for the War*.[346] A month later on February 9 Mrs. S. Falk appeared in a Dramatic Club amateur presentation of *Retribution*. She had acted in German speaking roles before but this was her first role in English.[347]

The Dramatic Club enlarged the Capital Hall stage and ordered $150 worth of "new and elegant scenery" painted by scenic artist L. L. Graham of Kansas City for its April 6 production of *The Woman in Red*.[348] Major Powell of the Boise Barracks directed and both of the Falks acted in major roles. Powell's transfer to the Dakotas in September hampered local dramatics for a time since he had supported and worked with theatre amateurs in Boise since 1886.

Amateurs retired from the stage until August 7 when soldiers from the Boise Barracks formed a minstrel troupe to present songs and a sketch, "The Wig Maker," that the press described as "immense."[349] On the night of September 12, the Schnabel sisters, seven young sisters from Boise, entertained with a musical concert.[350] Relief Engine Company One presented the last show, amateur or professional, of the 1888 season. On November 20 the "fire laddies,""with the help of Dr. O. L. Moore as director and actor, presented *Dearer Than Life*.[351]

Richards and Pringle's Georgia Minstrels played on February 20 to open the city's professional entertainment season.[352] Not until April 27 did the next professional troupe come to town. On that date the Harrison and Rogers Magnificent Company presented *My Geraldine* and closed its brief season the next night with *The*

Paymaster. Described in the paper as "better than Boise is used to," the troupe did poor business when Boise theatre-goers saved their money to attend the juvenile opera company advertised to follow Harrison and Rogers.[353] Unfortunately for all concerned, the juvenile opera company cancelled its engagement when its producers could not win a guarantee of $400 per night from local managers.

Miss Adele Payne and her company of eighteen men and five women performed on the last two days of June in productions of *The Wages of Sin* and *Oliver Twist* that won rave reviews from the press.[354] Just three days later, on July 3, George Wessell's Dramatic Company opened a three-show season with *The Black Flag* that also served as its offering for a special July 4 matinee. On the evening of Independence Day Wessell offered *The Danites*. The Wessell troupe "caught on" with Boise audiences and Capital Hall managers Hammond and Taylor "at great expense" secured the company for an additional three performances during which time the eleven member troupe presented *White Slave, Among the Pines* and a repetition of *The Black Flag.*[355]

Remarks in the *Statesman* about audience behavior at the DeMoss Family concerts on August 1 and 2 drew more interest than the actual performance. The editor advised manager Taylor, "the Capital Hall man," to "thin out [the] audience with a club." He felt that "silly girls and soft young men should reserve their clatter of silly nothings for the privacy of the parlor . . . ." He concluded his essay on theatrical manners: "It is not in good taste to make a stampede for the door in the middle of the last number on the performance. It is neither tony nor proper."[356]

The DeMoss Concert and already noted amateur productions concluded the 1888 entertainment events. As the year closed, amateur performers continued to prepare an often postponed production of *Noeime*. About this time a proclamation announcing the formal dedication of the Sonna Opera House appeared in the

Interior of Sonna's Opera House
Idaho State Historical Society 72-28.13

December 26 edition of the *Statesman*. Everything seemed to be in place for a banner theatre year in 1889. For the first time Boise had access to both a railroad to bring in touring combinations and a fine new opera house for its eager theatre patrons.

1889

The theatre season of 1889 began auspiciously with the dedication of the Sonna Opera House on January 4 before a large crowd of 450 local citizens. Speeches by local dignitaries lauded Peter Sonna for making an effort to offer Boise a proper opera house. Mr. Sonna appointed James A. Pinney, who had been familiar with theatre operations since his Idaho City days, as manager of the Sonna Opera House and Dr. O. L. Moore, who had many times served the city as director of local amateur theatricals, as stage

Sonna's Opera House
Idaho State Historical Society
71-162.1

manager. For the opening night show the Boise Amateur Dramatic Company offered a bill of *Noemie* or *The Daughter's Return* plus *Turn Him Out.*[357]

In the ensuing months of 1889 the number of entertainments performed in Boise equaled or surpassed those of any previous year. Only in 1866 and 1871 did Boiseans have the opportunity to attend thirty or more shows in a single year but in those years only one or two troupes presented most of the amusements. In 1889 over twenty different professional and amateur groups paraded before the Boise public. All but four performances took place in the Sonna Opera House.

The Irish comedian, J. S. Murphy, became the first professional actor to tread the boards of the Sonna Opera House when he and his company appeared in a matinee of *Kerry Gow* and an evening performance of *Shaun Rue* on January 19. He and his leading lady, Annie Mortland, played to crowded houses in the professional initiation of Boise's newest theatre.[358]

The Pocatello Dramatic Club, under the direction of Edwin Francis, traveled to Boise on January 26 in a specially scheduled train to demonstrate its talents before a local audience in *Above the Clouds*, a play produced with some success earlier in the Gate City. The amateur company, "composed of the best society people of Pocatello," also brought Professor Kay's orchestra that was "said to be the best on the Pacific coast."[359] After the performance cast, orchestra and audience joined in a night of social dancing.

Local Boise performers under the name of the Idaho Amateur Dramatic Club took their turn at pleasing Boise audiences with performances of *The Confederate Spy* on February 8 and 9 as a benefit for the G.A.R. relief fund. Play director O. L. Moore, assisted by Professor J. W. Daniels, enlisted the aid of twenty soldiers from Company "G" of the Boise Barracks for a scene in which they performed "the celebrated and magnificent bayonet drill."[360] The mixture of civilian and military talent drew fair houses to witness one of the best amateur plays seen in Boise up to that time.

One of the most famous actor-managers of the intermountain west, John S. Lindsay, paid the first of what would be many visits to Boise on February 21. During a short engagement of three days he produced *Ingomar, the Barbarian, Hazel Kirke*

John Lindsay
Utah Historical Society
Th12345

and *Damon and Pythias*, all of which attracted large audiences. The paper regarded the troupe as excellent, writing that "acting is the draw." Lindsay as Damon "gave evidence of talent of the very highest order."[361] Other performers mentioned in reviews were Mrs. Luella Lindsay, Mrs. Clomenia Pratt Bailey, Hyde and Rodgers. Lindsay's company planned to play two nights when it returned to Boise on

April 19. In spite of his previous success and the adulation of the press, only a small audience greeted the opening night performance of *Lady of Lyons*. Lindsay cancelled plans for a second show and left town. In view of Lindsay's cool reception, the *Statesman* warned "Boise City is losing its reputation for being a first-class show town."[362]

On March 9 the Sonna Opera House hosted Lydia Thompson and her "own grand Burlesque Company," a cast of

Lydia Thompson
University of Washington
Libraries Special Collections
Ph Coll 59.530

fifty-five artists in a vehicle called *Penelope*. Miss Thompson had been famous in American theatre since 1868 when she and her "British Blondes" burlesque company came to New York from London. The stiff admission charge of a dollar and a half for *Penelope* prevented few from attending the show. Miss Thompson not only drew a big crowd but caused a newspaperman to create a somewhat snide review. Recalling that he had seen Lydia Thompson many years before, the reviewer unkindly remarked, "Then she was fair to behold, but the hand of Father Time has lain heavily upon her and her short-lived beauty passed away" and that she wore "trappings which in the olden time would have caused her blonde hairs to stand on end."[363] The review ended on a positive note, however. Perhaps the author remembered that earlier in her career Miss Thompson had publicly thrashed the editor of the *Chicago Times* with a horsewhip for his attack on the supposed immorality of her performances.[364]

Richards and Pringle's Georgia Minstrels again amused Boise's population with well attended shows on March 25 and 26. The press couldn't deny the popularity of the troupe but found fault with the inclusion of Dutch and Irish songs in a minstrel show.[365]

Miss Belle Inman, advertised as "late leading lady with Modjeska," starred in Love-Inman Company's attractions on April 9 and 10.[366] Although the company's advertising promoted *Facing the Enemy* as the opening show of a brief engagement, the management substituted *Diamonds and Pearls*. It turned out that the former play employed local military men to "greater effect" and that troupers from the Boise Barracks would not be available until April 10, hence the substitution of the latter play. After all the publicity efforts, *Facing the Enemy* played to a "slim house" prompting the press to remark that Boise's theatre public "lost a rare treat" by not attending.[367]

Shortly after Miss Idaho and Miss Columbia of Boise's Schnabel family gave a concert on April 18,[368] the Stuttz New York Theatrical Company returned for performances on April 23 and 24.

While in Boise, J. G. Stuttz furnished Mr. Sonna with plans for remodeling his opera house. Stuttz suggested adding a gallery and parquette with raised seats and added that "acoustic properties of the hall" should "engage attention."[369] Mr. Sonna heeded most of the advice given by Stuttz and engaged architect James King to draw up plans and supervise the improvements. Work that began on May 1 to raise the seats from stage to back of the hall and to install a gallery was completed by July.[370]

Performances of *Lucretia Borgia* and *Crystal Cross* by the Stuttz Company proved popular with the public. Mr. Stuttz, with Elodie Alma as Lucretia, "drew forth storms of applause time and time again" from an "audience not used to tragedy."[371] The paper hailed the excellent support provided by the company for Stuttz, the magnificent costumes and the scenery "gotten up in the highest style."[372]

Capital Hall temporarily came back into use for performances as the Sonna Opera House underwent remodeling. A local language group headed by Mrs. Herschkel presented readings and declamations there on April 29. A small but talented traveling group, the John H. Oakes Comedy Sketch Club, appeared on May 7. Professor Harmon, magician and ventriloquist, renewed his acquaintance with Boise citizens in a show on July 13.[373]

With the completion of remodeling, the Sonna Opera House once again housed a variety of amateur and professional shows. Any acoustical faults noticed by critics last winter had been completely cured. A newspaper item assured the public "that a whisper can be heard from the stage in any part of the hall."[374] An amateur group tested the improved acoustics with a complimentary concert on July 24 for the members of the Constitutional Convention then in session at Boise.[375]

By August 16 professional theatre returned with the Frank Sanger Company in *A Bunch of Keys*. A fair sized audience responded well to the play and the company manager returned the compliment by stating that the Sonna Opera House was the best opera house on the Pacific coast outside of San Francisco.[376]

Local singer and instructor of song and dance, Madame Medini, directed her pupils and other amateurs in a performance of *Laila* on August 20. On November 20 the same Madame Medini appeared in a one-woman show of some two hours duration and received an extravagantly flattering review for her performance as a monologist. Following this success, she announced plans to tour to North Idaho, Portland, Spokane and other communities.[377]

The Farini-Mahon Circus drew little attention when it played Boise on September 2 and 3. The same held true for a single performance of *One of the Brave* by the Charles McCarthy Company on September 7. The McGinley Comedy Company gained some recognition in the press for its appearance on September 19. Robert and Eva McGinley, part of the Idaho pioneer theatre family, featured "classic triple tonguing cornet solos" by Walter and Lillie Fearn.[378] Although the paper felt that the show deserved better patronage, only a fair-sized audience showed up.

Several weeks passed before the next performance. Amateurs organized another dramatic club and dutifully announced that plays were in rehearsal but somehow they failed to meet announced performance dates. Then, Lew Johnson's Refined Colored Minstrels came to town for performances on November 11 and 12. Twenty "Renowned Artists" made up the Johnson company whose publicity emphasized "Genuine Plantation Specialties."[379] After a successful reception in Boise, the troupe went east to Mountain Home.

The theatrical season ended in December with two professional presentations. A stage version of *Around the World in Eighty Days* by the famous Kiralfy Company advertised to perform on December 7 and a troupe with the intriguing name of The Postage Stamp Comedy Company played in *A Social Season* to a full house on December 16. The press characterized the latter show as great musical entertainment by a company of real talent, especially the band.[380]

At the end of over a quarter of a century , Boise at last had elements in place to become a true "show town"—a suitable theatre venue in the Sonna Theatre, a secure if slightly indirect railroad connection for traveling theatre productions and a population eager to patronize professional performances. The lean years of cultural deprivation were at an end and a new era for theatrical entertainments in Boise had begun.

CHAPTER 3 NOTES

253 *Idaho Tri-Weekly Statesman.*, January 8, 1880, p. 3.; January 13, 1880, p. 3; January 20, 1880, p. 2; January 29, 1880, p. 3; February 14, 1880, p. 3.

254 *Ibid.*, March 6, 1880, p. 3.

255 *Ibid.*, November 13, 1880, p. 3; November 16, 1880, p. 3; November 23, 1880, p. 3; December 25, 1880, p. 3.

256 *Ibid.*, January 13, 1880, p. 3.

257 *Ibid.*, January 13, 1880, p. 3; January 29, 1880, p. 3.

258 *Ibid.*, January 20, 1880, p. 3; January 24, 1880, p. 3.

259 *Ibid.*, February 14, 1880, p. 3; March 6, 1880, p. 3.

260 *Ibid.*, September 30, 1880, p. 3; October 2, 1880, p. 3; October 5, 1880, p. 3; October 19, 1880, p. 3.

261 *Ibid.*, November 2, 1880, p. 3.

262 *Ibid.*, November 23, 1880, p. 3; November 27, 1880, p. 3.

263 *Ibid.*, December 25, 1880, p. 3.

264 *Ibid.*, January 1, 1881, p. 3.

265 *Ibid.*, April 21, 1881, p.3.

266 *Ibid.*, January 20, 1881, p. 3; April 2, 1881, p. 3.

267 *Ibid.*, February 26, 1881, p. 3; March 1, 1881, p. 3; April 14, 1881, p. 3; April 19, 1881, p. 3.

268 *Ibid.*, January 3, 1882, p. 3; February 2, 1882, p. 3; December 26, 1882, p. 3.

269 *Ibid.*, May 4, 1882, p. 3.

270 *Ibid.*, May 30, 1882, p. 3.

271 *Ibid.*, May 25, 1882, p. 3; May 27, 1882, p. 3; May 30, 1882, p. 3; June 27, 1882, p. 3.

272 *Ibid.*, June 6, 1882, p. 3.

273 *Ibid.*, August 5, 1882, p. 2; August 8, 1882, p. 3; August 12, 1882, p. 3; August 15, 1882, p. 3; August 17, 1882, p. 3; August 19, 1882, p. 3.

274 *Ibid.*, August 22, 1882, p. 2; August 24, 1882, p. 3.

275 *Ibid.*, September 5, 1882, p. 5; September 7, 1882, p. 5; September 21, 1882, p. 5.

276 *Ibid.*, September 23, 1882, p. 5.

277 *Ibid.*, September 30, 1882, p. 5; October 3, 1882, p. 5; October 7, 1882, p. 5; October 10, 1882, p. 5.

278 *Ibid.*, November 17, 1882, p. 3; November 25, 1882, p. 3; November 28, 1882, p. 3; December 5, 1882, p. 3; December 7, 1882, p. 3.

279   *Ibid.*, December 14, 1882, p. 3; December 19, 1882, p. 2.
280   *Ibid.*, January 18, 1883, p. 3; January 25, 1883, p. 3; January 30, 1883, p. 3.
281   *Ibid.*, January 30, 1883, p. 3; February 22, 1883, p. 3; February 27, 1883, p. 3; March 15, 1883, p. 3; March 17, 1883, p. 3; March 20, 1883, p. 3; March 22, 1883, p. 3; March 29, 1883, p. 3; April, 3, 1883, p. 3.
282   *Ibid.*, June 5, 1883, p. 3; June 12, 1883, p. 3.
283   *Ibid.*, June 19, 1883, p. 2; June 23, 1883, p. 3; July 3, 1883, p. 3; July 7, 1883, p. 3
284   *Ibid.*, August 30, 1883, p. 3.
285   *Ibid.*, September 13, 1883, p. 3.
286   *Ibid.*, August 30, 1883, p. 3; September 1, 1883, p. 3.
287   *Ibid.*, September 20, 1883, p. 3.
288   *Ibid.*, October 4, 1883, p. 3.
289   *Ibid.*, October 2, 1883, p. 3; October 4, 1883, p. 3.
290   *Ibid.*, October 6, 1883, p. 3; October 11, 1883, p. 3; October 13, 1883, p. 3; October 16, 1883, p. 3.
291   *Ibid.*, October 18, 1883, p. 3.
292   *Ibid.*, November 29, 1883, p. 3.
293   *Ibid.*, January 26, 1884, p .3.
294   *Ibid.*
295   *Ibid.*, January 10, 1884, p. 3; January 19, 1884, p. 3; January 22, 1884, p. 3; January 26, 1884, p. 3; January 29, 1884, p. 3; January 31, 1884, p. 3; February 2, 1884, p. 3.
296   *Ibid.*, July 24, 1884, p. 3.
297   *Ibid.*, July 26, 1884, p. 3.
298   *Ibid.*, July 29, 1884, p. 3.
299   *Ibid.*, July 31, 1884, p. 3.
300   *Ibid.*, August 7, 1884, p. 3.
301   *Ibid.*, September 20, 1884, p. 3.
302   *Ibid.*, September 23, 1884, p. 3.
303   *Ibid.*, July 1, 1884, p.3.
304   *Ibid.*, July 3, 1883, p. 3.
305   *Ibid.*, August 14, 1884, p. 3.
306   *Ibid.*, June 26, 1884, p. 3.
307   *Ibid.*
308   *Ibid.*, February 23, 1884, p. 3; February 25, 1884, p. 3; February 28, 1884, p. 3.

309 *Ibid.*, March 11, 1884, p. 3; March 13, 1884, p. 3.

310 *Ibid.*, April 10, 1884, p. 3; April 17, 1884, p. 3; April 22, 1884, p. 3.

311 *Ibid.*, December 9, 1884, p. 3; December 11, 1884, p. 3.

312 *Ibid.*, January 17, 1885, p. 2; January 20, 1885, p. 3; January 22, 1885, p. 3.

313 *Ibid.*, January 29, 1885, p. 3; February 7, 1885, p. 3.

314 *Ibid.*, February 7, 1885, p. 3; February 10, 1885, p. 3; February 12, 1885, p. 3.

315 *Ibid.*, March 12, 1885, p. 3.

316 *Ibid.*, March 14, 1885, p. 3.

317 *Ibid.*, April 9, 1885, p. 2; April 11, 1885, p. 3; April 18, 1885, p. 3.

318 *Ibid.*, May 14, 1885, p. 3.

319 *Ibid.*

320 *Ibid.*, June 23, 1885, p. 3.

321 *Ibid.*, July 14, 1885, p. 3.

322 *Ibid.*, August 25, 1885, p. 3.

323 *Ibid.*, November 24, 1885, p. 3.

324 *Ibid.*

325 *Ibid.*, November 28, 1885, p. 3.

326 *Ibid.*, September 15, 1885, p. 3; October 15, 1885, p. 3.

327 *Ibid.*, August 28, 1886, p. 3; September 22, 1886/ p. 3.

328 *Ibid.*, October 23, 1885, p. 3.

329 *Ibid.*, December 11, 1886, p. 3; December 16, 1886, p. 3.; December 23, 1886, p. 3; December 25, 1886, p. 3.

330 *Ibid.*, January 4, 1887, p. 4.

331 *Ibid.*, January 11, 1887, p. 3; January 15, 1887, p. 3.

332 *Ibid.*, February 17, 1887, p. 3.

333 *Ibid.*, March 24, 1887, p. 3.

334 *Ibid.*, April 23, 1887, p. 3.

335 *Ibid.*

336 *Ibid.*, June 4, 1887, p. 3.

337 *Ibid.*, June 23, 1887, p. 2.

338 *Ibid.*, July 30, 1887, p. 3; August 2, 1887, p. 3.

339 *Ibid.*, August 25, 1887, p. 3.

340 *Ibid.*, September 15, 1887, p. 2.

341 *Idaho Daily Statesman* (Boise), October 4, 1888, p. 3.

342 *Ibid.*, November 18, 1888, p. 3.

343 *Ibid.*, July 8, 1888, p. 3.

344 *Ibid.*

345 *Ibid.*, September 11, 1888, p. 3; September 28, 1888, p. 3.

346 *Ibid.*, January 10, 1888, p. 3.

347 *Ibid.*, February 11, 1888, p. 3.

348 *Ibid.*, April 24;, 1888, p. 2.

349 *Ibid.*, August 7, 1888, p. 3.

350 *Ibid.*, September 12, 1888, p. 3; September 14, 1888, p. 3.

351 *Ibid.*, November 18, 1888, p. 3; November 22, 1888, p. 3.

352 *Ibid.*, February 19, 1888, p. 2.

353 *Ibid.*, April 28, 1888, p. 3.

354 *Ibid.*, June 26, 1888, p. 2; June 28, 1888, p. 3; July 1, 1888, p. 3.

355 *Ibid.*, July 1, 1888, pp. 2,3; July 3, 1888, p. 3; July 5, 1888, pp 2,3; July 6, 1888, p. 3; July 7, 1888, p. 3.

356 *Ibid.*, August 3, 1888, p. 3.

357 *Ibid.*, January 2, 1889, p. 3; January 5, 1889, p. 3; January 6, 1889, p. 3.

358 *Ibid.*, January 17, 1889, p. 2; January 20, 1889, p. 3.

359 *Ibid.*, January 20, 1889, p. 3.

360 *Ibid.*, February 8, 1889, p. 3.

361 *Ibid.*, February 24, 1889, p. 3.

362 *Ibid.*, April 21, 1889, p. 3.

363 *Ibid.*, March 12, 1889, p. 3.

364 Lloyd Morris, *Curtain Time* (New York: Random House, 1953), p. 233.

365 *Idaho Daily Statesman*, March 27, 1889, p. 3.

366 *Ibid.*, April 4, 1889, p. 3.

367 *Ibid.*, April 11, 1889, p. 3.

368 *Ibid.*, April 18, 1889, p. 3.

369 *Ibid.*, April 26, 1889, p. 3.

370 *Ibid.*, April 27, 1889, p. 3; June 27, 1889, p. 3.

371 *Ibid.*, April 26, 1889, p. 3.

372 *Ibid.*

373 *Ibid.*, April 28, 1889, p. 2; May 2, 1889, p. 3; May 3,1889, p. 3; May 8 1889, p. 3; July 12, 1889, p. 3.

374 *Ibid.*, June 27, 1889, p. 3.

375 *Ibid.*, July 23, 1889, p. 3.

376 *Ibid.*, August 13, 1889, p. 3; August 18, 1889, p. 3.

377 *Ibid.*, August 9, 1889, p. 3; August 15, 1889, p. 3; August 20, 1889, p. 3; November 17, 1889, p. 3; November 20, 1889, p. 3; November 24, 1889, p. 3.

378 *Ibid.*, September 14, 1889, p. 3.

379 *Ibid.*, November 6, 1889, p. 3.

380   *Ibid.*, November 26, 1889, p. 3; December 10, 1889, p. 3; December 14, 1889, p. 3; December 18, 1889, p. 3.

CHAPTER 4

End of the Century

Boise, Idaho: 1890-1899

The number as well as the quality of theatrical entertainments available to Boise audiences grew markedly in the years between the opening of the Columbia Theatre and the end of the nineteenth century.   As of 1899 the number of entertainments presented in Boise had increased to almost 100, roughly four times that of amusements available in 1894. True to pattern, a large, well-equipped playhouse, a reliable railroad service and an increasing population fostered the growth of the capital city as a "show town." Nampa, Caldwell, Weiser and Payette, Idaho also developed theatres that attracted a few touring companies, usually regional or smaller troupes, but Boise continued to dominate the theatrical scene in southwest Idaho.

1890

The form of the 1890 theatrical year resembled that of the previous year as about a dozen different production organizations presented nearly thirty entertainments of various kinds including minstrel shows, circuses and dramatic presentations. Except for one circus, all performances took place at the Sonna Opera House.

Amateurs offered only three shows, the first a performance of a popular schoolroom burlesque titled *Deestrick Skule* on May 10.[381]   A concert by Lizzie Agnew and friends on September 26 featured songs from *Bohemian Girl* and dramatic delivery of a scene from *Leah* "with red fire and slow curtain."[382] As a benefit for the Parsonage Rectory Fund, Boise businessmen sponsored the

"Merchant's Carnival" on October 31 consisting of a musical concert and a style show.[383]

Seven different touring dramatic troupes produced most of the entertainment for the year. Charlotte Thompson and her company began the year with performances of *Jane Eyre* and *East Lynne* on January 6 and 7. Large houses and enthusiastic receptions that greeted these productions encouraged the company to add an additional performance on January 8.[384]

Charlotte Thompson
University of Washington
Libraries, Special Collections
PH Coll 75.539

Dan Sullivan's New Irish Comedy Company played "the latest San Francisco comedy," *Kitty from Cork*, on March 6, repeated it at the next day's matinee and then appeared in *Blarney* on March 7. Sullivan advertised that the first production used $5,000 of scenery depicting panoramic scenes of famous and historic Irish buildings. The show had some educational appeal, for public school students made up most of the audience for the second performance. Sullivan's singing of "McGinty," dances and "comicalities" no doubt enlivened the student's "lesson" for the evening.[385]

Daniel Bandmann, "the great tragedian," brought productions of Shakespearean plays to Boise for the first time since the 1860's when he and his company appeared for three nights in early March. His *Hamlet* on March 10 attracted a large and appreciative audience that filled both the parquet and gallery of the Sonna Opera House. The press applauded Bandmann and his excellent support finding special merit in the "closet scene" which was acted in so compelling a manner that one "could have heard a pin drop."[386] *The Merchant of Venice* on the following night with Bandmann's "new interpretation of Shylock" also met with financial and artistic success.[387] Bandmann completed his engagement with a production of *Othello* on March 12 but the event elicited no comment from the *Statesman*. The paper did comment that the Sullivan and Bandmann troupes had performed for a total of six successive nights to good houses and wondered if the miners wintering over in Boise might not come out poor in the spring due to attending so many plays.[388]

Daniel Bandmann
University of Washington
Libraries Special Collections
PH Coll 75.22

But miners escaped possible penury: the next theatrical production did not show up for ten weeks. Then, on May 23, the Katie Emmett Company paused in town for one night to present *The Waifs of New York*.[389] Three months passed before the next attraction played Boise. On August 27 the Wade-LeRoyle Musical Comedy Company, on tour in Idaho for the second time, stopped in Boise to produce a double bill of *What Is It?* and a "sparkling burlesque," *Robinson Crusoe and His Man Friday*. Lottie Wade, the principal star, gained press recognition as "an artist of considerable versatility."[390] Two months later, on October 27, the Royce-Lansing Comedy Company experienced a "decided success" with its rendition of *Tom's Vacation*.[391]

A week's engagement by the Vincent Comedy Company, commencing on November 3, ended the cavalcade of touring dramatic troupes for the 1890 season. Felix and Eva Vincent headed the company that also included J. D. Bernard, Harry Blanchard and others. Vincent's productions offered little novelty in terms of repertoire with such old standards as *The Serious Family* and *The Swiss Cottage* but the press treated the company favorably, finding productions "admirably" and "respectably" presented with negative comments reserved for the cold temperatures in the theatre on nights of performance.[392]

Boise audiences had several opportunities to attend non-dramatic entertainments in 1890. Three minstrel shows came to town between May and September. W. S. Cleveland's Magnificent Minstrels with "Forty-six Heroes of Two Hemispheres" arrived early enough on May 14 to give the traditional minstrel parade in the afternoon before the show.[393] The parade, usually employed to attract publicity for a minstrel show, seemed pointless to the press in view of the fact that almost all tickets had been sold before the troupe came to town. Audience expectations were met and Cleveland's Minstrels pleased a capacity house. The twenty-five artists of McCabe and Young's Operatic Minstrels played on July 11 but the press ignored their efforts.[394] The same happened again when the McCandless Colored Minstrels were booked by James Pinney for September 20.[395]

One relatively large circus and one dog and pony show, visited Boise in the summer of 1890. The press reported little of McFlynn's Circus during its Boise

Gentry Brothers
James Gentry Memorial
www.findgrav.com

engagement on June 17; however, the *Statesman* did carry a story about the near panic or disaster that occurred in Caldwell when a windstorm struck the circus tent. Fortunately, no injuries or permanent harm resulted.[396] The Gentry Brother's Dog and Pony Show occupied the Sonna Opera House on August 2. Gentry offered this popular children's attraction for years and eventually formed three such companies that toured simultaneously.[397]

A pantomime troupe and an elocutionist completed the variety of offerings for 1890. On November 18 a troupe with the ungainly title, Hanlon-Volter-Martinetti Company, performed its variety entertainments before an absolutely packed house of Boise, Nampa and Caldwell citizens. As one part of the evening's entertainment, the company presented Marinetti in "A Scene in the Snow," a performance in pantomime—a rarity for Boise patrons up to that time. The company, described as an English pantomime and novelty company, also featured German athletes, including one lady with a "pretty face and form like Venus" who carried four others about the stage—a weight of 550 pounds. Other acts involved the Wartenberg family of gymnasts and Walter Emerson, cornetist with the famous Gilmore band. Due to the limitations of the opera house stage, the trapeze act couldn't be performed. After the troupe left for Pocatello, the paper wrote that such entertainment had "never been equaled here."[398] As the final entertainment of the year, the *Statesman* briefly noted the presence of Professor E .K. Webber on December 29—an elocutionist who performed with unnamed others.[399]

1891

The theatre season of 1891 generally imitated the pattern of the previous two years in terms of the number of dramatic and other forms of entertainment offered. Again many groups, about seventeen, engaged in presenting just over thirty shows, all in the Sonna Opera House except for a circus performance. Three amateur groups appeared in six evenings of amusements during the year. Eight professional dramatic companies presented most of the entertainments. The remaining troupes offered the usual variety of minstrel shows, concerts, etc.

The Idaho Dramatic Company mounted the first two amateur productions in January and February of 1891. They chose to present *The Confederate Spy* on January 21 and enlisted the aid of soldiers Company "A" of the Idaho National Guard to present a " brilliant bayonet drill" plus musicians from the Boise Juvenile Brass Band who dressed in their new uniforms to perform in the show.[400] The local dramatic company stuck to its military theme and presented *Soldier of Fortune* on February 13 under the direction of John Barry. The show received an unusual, highly negative review. Although some actors collected accolades, the reviewer attacked the play as a "trashy, weak production" suffering from "lack of . . . preparation" and miscasting of performers.[401]

The Salt Lake Home Dramatic Company fared much better with the Boise theatre public in its performances on February 18 and 19. This much heralded company of seventeen performers had acted together for several years. During its first Boise engagement large audiences turned out for the troupe's performances of *Confusion* and *Young Mrs. Winthrop*. The company also won the good opinion of the press that characterized the group as good actors who did not strain for effect and avoided artificiality.[402]

Near the end of the year local singers and actors formed the Boise Opera Company to present Gilbert and Sullivan's *Patience* on December 16 and 17. Evidently the faults that marred previous amateur efforts had been corrected, for the comic opera production received a sympathetic review from the press.[403]

Professional theatre companies did not perform in Boise until April of 1891. Manager Pinney of the Sonna Opera House had some difficulty booking shows due to problems with the railroad schedule. When Pinney announced a list of coming attractions in the March 24 edition of the *Statesman*, the paper quoted him as saying he would get "the cream of traveling companies" if the Union Pacific put on two trains a day each way "as the new time table would get them in and out of here without losing a day, as is now the case."[404] Unfortunately for Pinney and the Boise public, the railroad did not schedule extra trains and none of Pinney's attractions listed for March ever played in Boise that month.

Kajanka, a ballet and scenic spectacular by the Miller Brothers' Company, came to Boise from Salt Lake City on April 4 with a troupe of thirty-five performers. As usual in such shows, a thin plot provided opportunities for the inclusion of acrobats, dancers and other "specialties." "Everything excellent" said the press even though the company showed to disadvantage upon so small a stage as the Sonna Opera House afforded.[405] *Kajanka* had never played in a town the size of Boise, which had only recently grown to a population of over 4,000.

John Dillon, a nationally recognized star comedian, also played in Boise in April. An impressive publicity campaign of ads and printed "puffs" resulted in a heavy advance ticket sale before Dillon appeared in his current vehicle, *Wanted the Earth*, on April 15. Dillon, a former brother-in-law of John Langrishe, a prominent Colorado and Montana actor-manager, began his career in the 1850's with Langrishe's Wisconsin troupe. After years as a local favorite in Chicago he went to New York and established himself as a character actor

John Dillon
Donated from Dillon Estate

and comedian. His annual national tours further enhanced his reputation as a comedy performer.[406]

McFadden's Uncle Tom's Cabin Company returned to Boise on May 9 to perform in a big white tent set up at the corner of Fort Street and "Lover's Lane." As in past seasons McFadden offered double everything: Two Marks, two

Uncle Tom's Cabin
en.wikipedia.com

Topsies, two donkeys, two well trained ponies, four bloodhounds, two special cars, ten musicians, twenty performers and six Tennessee Jubilee singers.[407] Newspapers regarded "Tom Shows" like McFadden's as too well known by the public to be worthy of review.

Three companies made it to Boise in June. Abbie Carrington's small, talented opera company sang *Rose of Castile* on June 15 for a rewardingly large group of auditors. George Thatcher's Minstrels followed closely on June 17 with a decidedly different style of music. E. B. Warman display his elocutionary talents in performances on June 29 and 30.[408]

The summer months passed before the next attraction arrived in the form of Adam Forepaugh's Circus which entertained on September 19.[409] Theatrical activity increased markedly during the rest of the month with an extended engagement of the Union Square Dramatic Company.

The Union Square players began a season of six evenings on September 21 with a production of *The Clemenceau Case*. The press commended the excellent acting of William Powers, Jennie Lee and Agnes Warden in support of stars Josephine Rodgers and Frederick Bock. In the next five nights the company offered a season of old favorites such as *The Willow Copse* and *Crimes of the Great City* plus an all but inevitable showing of *East Lynne*. After its departure the press wrote that the company's final production, Dion Boucicault's *Streets of New York*, had been its best show.[410]

Only three entertainments graced the month of October. Cosgrove and Grant charged a dollar and a half for their show, *The Dazzler*, when it hit town on October 10. For the admission price the management guaranteed the audience no less than ten soubrettes, twenty comedians, twenty others and Bonnie Kate Castleton as the star. The Cleveland Minstrels paid a return visit on October 26 and the Innes Band, a famous musical organization, gave a concert on October 29.[411]

November was devoid of both professional and amateur diversions but December turned out to be a fruitful month for audiences when two troupes presented ten evenings of plays. On December 19 the Fowler and Warmington Company's production of *Skipped by the Light of the Moon* occupied the Sonna stage.[412] Two nights later the Chicago Comedy Company opened in *Lynwood* with an old Boise favorite, Frank Cleaves, returning after an absence of almost ten years. M. B. "Goldie" Goldstein managed the troupe that also included Miss Lizzie Lingham, Horace Ewing, Imogene Abel, Sutherland, Miss Margaret Goldie, W. E. Allen, Kay, Lutherance and Ober. The troupe played nightly through December 26 to good business and generally favorable reviews. The season featured Frank Cleaves' specialties, *Davey Crockett and Shingawn*. After a short vacation, the troupe gave a final benefit performance of *The French Spy* on December 30 for the G.A.R.'s new hall. Shortly after the first of the year the company departed for the east.[413]

1892

Theatrical presentations rose slightly in number during 1892 as did the number of professional companies visiting Idaho's capital city. Twenty professional companies and two amateur groups presented thirty-seven various forms of entertainment, all but three at the Sonna Opera House. For the first time in years, no circus came to town. Boiseans witnessed few amateur productions in 1892. A local entertainment at the G.A.R. Hall on February 24 evoked little comment in the paper; however, the press displayed marked enthusiasm for the Salt Lake City Home Dramatic Company upon its second visit to Boise on April 18 and 19. An item of great length dealt with the background of some of the amateur performers and revealed that Mr. Wells of the company once ran for mayor of Salt Lake City, Spencer owned a large shoe store and Young was a grandson of the famous Mormon leader, Brigham Young. H. G. Whiting, head of the *Salt Lake City Herald*, served as manager of the troupe. Others in the troupe also had close connections with the social, business and religious life of Salt Lake City. The press described audiences for the company's productions of *Held by the Enemy* and *Esmerelda* as "brilliant" and rendered ever so flattering reviews of the visiting troupe's talents. The Boise Philharmonic Orchestra aided the efforts of the visiting company by playing selections between acts.[414]

May Irwin and company led off an impressive procession of eighteen professional traveling companies that stopped off in Boise during 1892 when they presented *Boys and Girls* on January 4. Advertised as the "most expensive attraction ever brought to Boise," the evening's "fun and nonsense attracted a large audience that thrilled to the talents of Miss Irwin. The *Statesman*, ever vigilant to protect the public, objected that "a little coarseness" crept in to the performance but did not specify the nature of the "coarseness."[415]

May Irwin
NYPL: Billy Rose Collection
TH-23488

Katie Putnam returned to Boise for the fourth time on February 22 to fill an engagement of four nights. She opened with *Love Finds a Way*, a play new to most Boiseans, but completed her stand with a tried and true repertoire of *Erma the Elf*, *The Old Curiosity Shop* and *Lena, the Madcap*. L.O. Hart, Robert Bell, Ada Fremont, Harry Colton, Charles Mortimer, Thomas Findlay, Rose Wilder, Max Fox, H. B. Emery, L. M. Edgar, J. C. Crowell, R. D. Willis, Harry Leslie, Edith Murry and Kate Fawcett acted in supporting roles. Large crowds attended each show before the company left to fill an engagement in Salt Lake City.[416]

Little appeared in print concerning a performance of *Dolly Varden* by Patti Rosa and company on March 12. The Beebe-Barbour Company gained only slightly more recognition for the seven plays it presented between April 11 and 16. Little Grace Beebe, "Child Wonder of the Dramatic World," and actor-playwright Edward Barbour opened with *A Legal Document*, an original play by Barbour. The troupe filled out the rest of its run with standard dramas of the day such as *Black Diamonds, Joe, the Waif* and *Peck's Bad Boy*.[417]

A series of one-night stand, "combination" attractions followed. On April 30 *Avenged*, a "tank drama" with Orson Clifford, taxed the resources of the Sonna Opera House with a scene requiring a real river of running water. In the scene a dog, Graff, rescues a drowning man. The play also required the services of two "acting horses" and three additional "acting dogs." The promise of such exciting action created a brisk demand for tickets.[418] A Frohman production of *All the Comforts of Home* played on May 2.[419]

Marie Wainwright and company offered Boucicault's society comedy, *London Assurance*, on May 18. The performance aroused the scorn of the local press as "another disappointment visited upon a Boise audience."[420] The critic accused the actors of just walking through their parts and butchering a strong play. He pointed out that a large and fashionable audience did its best to honor Miss

Wainwright but saw "a feeble effort" on her part to return the compliment. Only Blanche Walsh, later to become a star in her own right, seemed to make any effort to please. On May 21 W. H. Powers' Company offered Irish reels, jig dancing and a singing quartet in its rendition of *The Ivy Leaf.* The drama itself depicted a terrifying scene in which an eagle carried away a live child in its talons![421]

Blanche Walsh
University of Washington Libraries Special Collections
SU-S-1252

Traveling combinations continued to play on the Sonna stage, now under the management of Bayhouse and Fritz. Former manager J.A. Pinney had left about April 25 to plan and build his own theatre. On May 28 the new managers booked *The Rivals*, a "Pantomimical Musical Comedy Extravaganza" that featured "The Lilliputians" with Mrs. General Tom Thumb and the "Parlor Vaudeville Phalanx" plus the "Royal Japs."[422] A few days later, on June 7, another "Magnificent Pantomime,' the Miller Brothers' *Kajanka*, returned to Boise with the Merlini Acrobats, the Mariposa Dancers, Ravel, the clown and the Serpentine Dance.[423] At the end of the month the W. H. Powers' Ivy Leaf Company again played Boise in *The Fairies' Well.*[424]

After the usual summer pause in theatrical activity, the season resumed on August 29 with a double bill by the Charles Frohman Company, *Gloriana* and *The Major's Appointment.* Almost seven weeks passed before the next dramatic presentations, seven plays by the Wilber Company. James R. McCann managed the troupe that starred himself and Lizzie Kendall. They opened an unremarkable series of standard melodramas on October 24 that closed on October 29. The season closed at the Sonna Opera House with the presentation of *Niobe* by Abbott and Teal's Comedy Company.[425]

Only a few non-dramatic entertainments played Boise during 1892. The famed Fisk Jubilee Singers gave a concert on April 26, Gorton's Famous New Orleans Minstrels packed the house for an exceptionally fine display of "Refined Minstrelsy" on July 14 and the Eden-Fontana Combination appeared at Boise's Natatorium on September 7 and 8 for an exhibition of mind reading,

James A. Pinney
Idaho State Historical Society
69.1081

hypnotism and rope tying.[426] About October 17 Earley's Standard Theatre, a "cozy place of amusement," opened in Boise to offer variety entertainments. Under the management of Billy Miln, the establishment promised "new stars every week."[427]

One last entertainment awaited the Boise public in 1892, the inaugural performance at Mayor James A. Pinney's new showplace, the Columbia Theatre. On December 12 the eminent American actress, Julia Marlowe, appeared as Rosalind in Shakespeare's pastoral comedy, *As You Like It.*[428]

Pinney had been well connected with Idaho theatrical enterprises in some way for more than a quarter century when he decided to build and manage his own theatre. In Idaho City during the 1860's he had been a partner in the second Idaho Theatre. After he moved to Boise, he sold theatre tickets in his bookshop. Pinney became the first manager of Sonna's Opera House in 1889 and conducted business with the traveling professional companies and local amateur organizations. With these varied experiences in his background he made public on May 27 in the *Statesman* his plans to build the Columbia Theatre.

Designed by the architectural firm of Paulsen and Lavelle and built by Alexander McPherson's local construction company, the

Columbia reportedly cost $35,000. Plans for the building, located on Eighth Avenue and Jefferson Street, called for dimensions of sixty feet wide by 122 feet deep with a gridiron height of some sixty feet that would handle scenery as large as sixteen by twenty-four feet. The spacious sixty foot square auditorium was designed to seat 500 with room for an equal number of seats available in the sixty by eighty foot balcony. Two tiers of box seats provided an added 28 seats. The stage measured an impressive forty feet deep by thirty feet wide with eight full sets of painted scenery, stage traps and a large orchestra pit. Four very wide aisles separated the main floor seating while the numerous exits secured safety and convenience. A "ladies' foyer" and a gentlemen's smoking room were located off the balcony level. Decorated in French renaissance style, the Columbia featured building materials of pressed brick, cut stone, hard wood, slate and cut glass. Two huge hot air furnaces provided necessary heating and 450 incandescent lamps illuminated the auditorium.[429]

Columbia Theatre
Idaho State Historical Society
70-1691

    Pinney's announcement of his plans to build the Columbia came just short of a month after press items appeared describing the efforts of Peter Sonna "and others" to erect a new opera house west of Sonna's block at a cost of $75,000. Architect King drew up plans for a theatre "bigger and better in every way" and intended to begin construction in the summer. After Pinney disclosed his intentions , the paper reported Peter Sonna as "not daunted by Pinney's plans to build a theatre" and that Sonna would go to Spokane to look at the Auditorium Theatre, the finest in the whole Northwest, presumably as a model for his own theatre plans. For whatever reasons, Sonna dropped his plans to build a competitive new theatre and stayed with his original opera house that continued to accommodate shows for over another decade.[430]

By July 23 the press carried accounts of the rapid progress being made on the construction of the Columbia Theatre, planned to be completed by December 1. Optimistically, Pinney had already engaged Clara Morris, a leading star of the day, for an early January date.[431] On November 23 Pinney publicized the opening night as December 12 at which time Julia Marlowe would appear in Shakespeare's pastoral comedy, *As You Like It*. When tickets sales began on December 5, Pinney and three others had already purchased the theatres four box seats. While workmen had been busy constructing and completing the theatre, Professor Robert Ballott was busily engaged in composing an overture, "Columbian Festival," for the Philharmonic Orchestra to play on opening night.[432]

Newspaper accounts of the Columbia Theatre's opening night include a description of the theatre decorations painted by Boise artist Max Kohn who "worked night and day to complete his great task." The drop curtain portrayed "a faithful water color reproduction of Wagner's magnificent 'Circus Maximus'" and above the proscenium arch Kohn depicted Mayor Pinney flanked by copies of "Fatima" on the left and "The Odalisque" on the right. The western curve of the frescoed ceiling featured portraits of Shakespeare, Beethoven, Liszt and Tennyson matched by pictures of Hugo, Goethe, Wagner and Mozart on the opposite side.[433]

Julia Marlowe
NYPL: Billy Rose
Collection
65601

The very eagerly anticipated opening night performance of *As You Like It* went off with "less hitch" than usually expected on such occasions. An overflowing house made up of the elite of Boise and surrounding towns filled the new theatre. The press praised Julia Marlowe for being "an ideal Rosalind" whose appearance "did honor to the event." The reviewer noted that "The constant play of her features kept the close attention of every one so that no expression might be lost" and claimed that "Those eyes shot darts from Cupid's bow that were felt far beyond the stage." Miss Marlowe enjoyed good support from Robert Taylor as Orlando, Giles Shine as Touchstone, Kittie Wilson as Audrey and H .A. Weaver, Sr. as Adam. But, according to the enthusiastic critic, it was the "laughing eyes and dimpled chin of Julia Marlowe" that the audience carried away in its memory.[434]

1893

At the close of the third decade of Idaho entertainment annals Boise audiences witnessed more shows (forty) by more groups (thirty-two) than ever before in the city's history. Variety in entertainments and in production groups marked a season when everything from opera to circus came to town presented by troupes ranging in size from a lone elocutionist to a large minstrel aggregation. Most all attractions played in the new Columbia Theatre except for the few amateur shows that were better suited for performance in the smaller space of the Sonna Opera House.

Six amateur entertainments presented at intervals throughout the year mirrored the variety provided by the professional touring companies. With Miss Roberts as their director, local students presented the operetta *Old Friends and New Faces* at the Sonna Opera House on January 10 with "decided success in every particular."[435] On May 12 students again appeared in another operetta, *Dan the Newsboy*—this time at the Columbia Theatre as a benefit for the kindergarten. A week later local ladies Mrs. Swift and Mrs. Andrus headed a "delightful" concert by Boise talent at the Sonna Opera House. The men of G.A.R. Hall, Post 4 celebrated Independence Day at the Columbia Theatre with their rendition of *The Spy of Atlanta* on July 3 and 4. The Agnew sisters gave a "rare musical and elocutionary treat" at Pinney's Columbia on September 29. Mrs. Alice Hamill Handcock appeared with local talent at the Sonna Opera House of December 15 in a program of recitations, Shakespearean impersonations and Delsartian poses.[436]

Reflecting a national theatrical trend toward more and more reliance on traveling "combination" troupes to provide dramatic entertainment, only one professional company played in Boise for more than one or two nights. Railroad routes for touring theatre enterprises had become well established through southern Idaho by 1893.

Combination companies played longer engagements, repeating the same play for several nights, in cities with sufficient population to sustain attendance. They preferred to make "hops" of no more than a hundred and fifty miles between smaller communities, playing one-night stands until reaching the next large city. Since Idaho had no large cities, companies played Salt Lake City for several nights, then "hopped" through Idaho to Pocatello and Boise before exiting to Baker, Oregon. Or companies reversed the order of playing in Idaho if traveling west to east. Some smaller, often regional, companies that still played in smaller communities off of main railroad lines would also play in Boise but their touring routes were less predictable.

Boise's parade of seventeen touring companies began with Inez Russell Montgomery on January 4 in her one-woman presentation of songs and recitations, a grand entertainment for a small but appreciative audience.[437] The much heralded talents of the celebrated Clara Morris drew a much larger but less appreciative audience when she appeared on January 9 in *Article 47*. A "large and brilliant assemblage" witnessed her in "acting below what is expected of her." The press viewed supporting players more favorably but felt Clara Morris in her last tour of the West "did not win the hearts of the audience."[438]

John Dillon, a hit the year before, returned for performances on January 11 and 12 in a new play, *A Model Husband*, and a repeat of last year's *Wanted the Earth*. His self-styled "laughing festival" fairly filled the Columbia Theatre with an audience convulsed in constant laughter by his antics, "his use of slang and of meaningless or inappropriate words being the main element of his mirth making."[439]

Clara Morris
University of
Washington Libraries
Special Collections
PH Coll 75.408

The four evening engagement of Katie Putnam from January 17 to 21 turned out to be the longest single run of the year in Boise. During her stay she abandoned her old, rather predictable, repertoire for some new works for her company, *An Unexpected Express Package*, *The Little Maverick*, and *Dad's Girl* but retained *Love Finds a Way* from previous seasons. Actors T. B. Findlay, H. B. Emery and J. J. Kelt of her company must have been unhappy with a local press opinion that the company had little to offer but Miss Putnam. Performances drew only fair audiences for a supposed Boise favorite who had played the town several times in the past nine years. At the end of the run Katie Putnam revealed that she was thinking of leaving the stage, a threat not made good for several years to come.[440]

Two perennial favorites received decidedly different receptions when they played Boise in late February. Atkinson Comedy Company's version of the extremely well known *Peck's Bad Boy* with Fred Wenzel and Maude Davis in leading roles warranted a vitriolic broadside from a *Statesman* reviewer who wrote: "It is a shame that such barnstorming monstrosities are allowed to stalk over the country palming themselves off on the unsuspecting public."[441] He hoped the audience would not let their disappointment at this production keep them away from the upcoming production of Denman Thompson's star vehicle, *The Old Homestead* — a play that Thompson himself performed before the American public for nineteen seasons. Heeding the concern of the critic, 900 Boise theatre-goers crowded the Columbia on February 27 to experience the simple humor and sentimentality of *The Old Homestead* as performed by the E. A. MacFarland Company. Clearly the play and its songs—"Old Oaken Bucket," "I Stood On the Bridge at Midnight" and "Rock-A-Bye-Baby"—made for a huge success that evening.[442]

After theatre patrons went without diversions during March, April offered only two shows. On April Fools' Day the celebrated actor E. H. Sothern, under the management of the equally celebrated Daniel Frohman, acted in *Captain Lettarblair*, an event largely ignored by the press except for the printing of publicity puffs in advance of the show.[443] The same indifference greeted Patti Rosa and her return showing of her jolly comedy, *Dolly Varden*, on April 26.[444]

James J. Corbett, the reigning heavyweight boxing

James J. Corbett
NYPL:Billy Rose Collection
TH-04820

champion of the world, starred in *Gentleman Jack* on May 5, a production that turned out to be the only dramatic offering for the month of May in Boise. As unlikely as it seems, Corbett spent his time between defenses of his heavy weight title touring in light comedies with his wife. Although his fame as a pugilist served to attract audiences, he more than held his own in the theatre as a skilled light comedian and made several national tours during his days

Mrs. Corbett
NYPL Billy Rose
Collection Th-04823

of fame. His productions were well mounted with superb scenic effects and handsome costumes, especially for his wife. *Gentleman Jack*, tailored to Corbett's double talents, naturally contained a fight scene. As if that were not enough of a display of his boxing prowess, to please his fans he donned the "mitts" and had a bout with a member of the company at the close of the performance. Corbett's popularity, the scarcity of dramatic offerings and extensive coverage in the press produced a tremendous rush on the box office before the engagement.[445] "Gentleman Jim" packed the house and pleased the public in *Gentleman Jack*.

Over two months passed before Robert Mantell and his company brought *Monbars* to the Columbia on July 14. Few companies toured in the summer at this time as farming and related business occupied a majority of the population. Summer heat in the days before reliable air conditioning also discouraged theatre-going. For these reasons, Mantell played before a small audience even though he offered a well-acted, powerful play.[446] Three days later George Thatcher and his Operatic Extravaganza Company presented a work titled *Africa* that required the talents of twenty-six principal singers and dancers plus a chorus of thirty-five.[447]

Newton Beers promised special scenery, new songs and new dances in the promotion for his September 4 production of *Lost in London*. His publicity failed to attract more than a small house. Adding insult to injury, the *Statesman* issued a scathing review stating what little merit the play possessed was "destroyed by inferior acting" on the part of Mr. Beers and his support who were "stiff" in their presentation of character. The critical diatribe ended

Mrs. John Drew
University of Washington
Libraries, Special Collections
PH Coll 59.171

with, "If they were ever 'Lost in London' well might last night's audience wish they had remained undiscovered."[448]

While Boise audiences endured many poor traveling productions, the excellent attractions that did come to town restored patron's confidence in theatre-going. Just such an attraction was Mrs. John Drew's October 13 production of Sheridan's *The Rivals* with Mrs. Drew as Mrs. Malaprop. Mrs. Drew (grand-mother of the famed Barrymores) deserved her reputation as a celebrated actress. Years before she had gained fame as the leading lady and manager of Philadelphia's Arch Street Theatre, one of America's finest theatres.[449] Her production of *The Rivals* had been on tour for several years so it came as no surprise that the local critic found the play "practically perfect in every detail, . . . a finished production that gives unalloyed pleasure."[450]

The final theatrical engagements of October met with contrasting receptions. A crowded house on October 16 witnessed the Frohman Company presentation of *The Girl I Left Behind Me*.

According to to a local reviewer the play had the proper mixture of entertainment elements; "There was a touch of pathos, a bit of comedy, and sufficient thrilling situations to make up a happy combination."[451] The Stuttz Company, returning to Boise after an absence of some years, did not fare as well with the public or press. A small house greeted the October 30 show, *La Bastille*, a performance that the press criticized for poor acting by all but Mr. Stuttz. Things went no better for the final show the next night.[452]

November's shows earned only brief mention in the local press. Italian actress Madeline Merli starred in *The Story of a Kiss* on November 6. The Fowler and Warmington Company performed *Skipped by the Light of the Moon* on November 24 and 25 before fair audiences.[453]

December's only engagement, two nights by the Calhoun Opera Company, closed the 1893 theatrical season. On December 27 a sizable audience enjoyed a "finished performance" of *The Mikado* with its fine leads and excellent chorus. *Black Hussar* on the next evening gave great satisfaction to another large audience.[454]

While theatrical troupes dominated the entertainment scene, Boise audiences also supported a variety of other entertainments. The Royal Japanese Company gave gymnastic exhibitions on February 15 and 16 of 1893. A week later the Boston Operatic Concert Company's concert with soloists Dolph and Susie Levino and Albert Hawthorn, basso, accompanied by the Great Vienna Lady Orchestra drew a fair audience for the "very high class entertainment."[455]

Minstrel shows remained popular in Boise. Primrose and West's Minstrels paraded and then performed on May 1. Their show, "clean and rich from beginning to end," attracted the "largest house yet" to the Columbia Theatre.[456] Boiseans greeted an appearance by the Barlow Brothers Mammoth Minstrels on December 3 with another full house. The press hailed the show as the "best to visit

Boise in years" and complimented the thirty minstrel artists for a "performance that was finished, chaste and withal uproariously funny."[457]

Miscellaneous entertainments included McIver Tyndall, a mind reader, medium and mesmerist, at the Columbia on May 13 and the Howard Athenaeum Star Specialty Company on May 29.[458] Sanger and Lent's International Allied Shows received mixed reviews for its circus on June 12. Although the pre-show parade was poor and marred by two runaway horses, the performance itself was good. The press objected to "vile red lemonade and dust" as well as misleading advertising and the lack of both aquarium features and adequate numbers of animals in the menagerie.[459] A December 15 concert by the Spokane Auditorium Orchestra concluded the non-dramatic entertainment of 1893.[460]

At the end of almost thirty years of theatrical history, Boise could boast of two fine theatres and a supportive public for entertainments of all kinds. The city needed better railroad scheduling and service to attract the better touring companies but this situation would be remedied in time. The availability of theatrical and other entertainments would grow and expand for another twenty years in the capital city of Idaho.

1894

As a reflection of the depressed state of the national economy in the previous year, Boise theatrical business declined to almost half of that of 1893. Even the growing awareness of the Columbia Theatre's existence among theatrical managers did little to improve matters and for a time Boise theatre development halted. Only twenty-six shows, almost all at the Columbia Theatre, interrupted the routine of life in Boise during 1894. The public saw fifteen plays, three minstrel shows, four concerts and four variety entertainments, all single evening engagements save one.

Attractions appeared rarely during the winter and early spring of 1894. The Howard Athenaeum Company gave the first and only January performance on the thirteenth. The variety entertainment pleased the public in spite of a disappointing effort by its star, Lottie Collins.[461] America's favorite Swede, the title character in *Ole Olson*, showed up on February 27 as the single offering for that month. Richard Baker in the title role, aided by actresses Olive Martin and Adelaide Crawford, delighted the large crowd in attendance at the familiar ethnic comedy.[462]

Theatres remained dark through March but in April two companies came to Boise. On April 9 a large house witnessed much uproar and "horseplay" when the Monroe Company presented *My Aunt Bridget* with George Monroe in the title role.[463] Sam Burton and Lillie Coleman offered a street parade before their presentation of *Si Perkins* on April 19. The press judged Burton and the music the only redeeming features in the production and found "nothing to the play and less to the players."[464]

Theatre business picked up in May when entertainers presented two concerts and a play. Miss Neally Stevens, "America's Greatest Lady Pianist," played at the Presbyterian Church on May 18 and W.H. Sherwood, "America's Greatest Pianist," presented a concert on May 31 with the assistance of local musicians.[465] Between piano concerts, the Morris and Emery Company gave two performances of *The World* on May 21 and 22. Harry Emery, who had appeared in Boise several times before, more than pleased the audience. So did the drama's exciting scenic effects that featured a sinking ship scene complete with lightning, wind and rain. Other attractions included comedy songs and dances along with scenes on a raft, at the harbor in Naples and in a lunatic asylum.[466]

June's entertainment events consisted of four shows. The Chicago Lady Quartet offered music and impersonations at a concert on June 2, attracting an audience much smaller than the group merited.[467] Thirty local entertainers made up the Coonville College Minstrel Company that appeared at the Columbia Theatre on June 12.[468] The press labeled Hopkin's Trans-Oceanic Star Specialty Company as the "best for some time, if ever" when this troupe performed on June 18.[469] Richard and Pringle's Georgia Minstrels closed the month's entertainments with a show on June 23 that featured Billy Kersands and a cake walk competition.[470]

The three shows presented in July and August varied greatly in quality. In July a general strike of railroad employees delayed the presentation of *Lady Windemere's Fan* by the Gustave Frohman Company until the eleventh. The press termed this production of Oscar Wilde's famous drama as one of the best ever given in Boise.[471] The much anticipated appearance of Mrs. Cora Potter and Kyrle Bellew in their production of *In Society* on August 15 disappointed the large Boise audience in attendance. The train arrived late with tired, hungry performers on board and Mrs. Potter in ill health, all of which contributed to a poor performance redeemed only by the acting of Mr. Bellew.[472] A less anticipated performer, Anna May Abbott,—the electrical wonder—gave a demonstration of her unique abilities at a show on August 28.[473]

Local talent and a new variety theatre provided the only entertainments in September. Local musicians attracted a large audience for their revival of the Coonville College Minstrels on September 18.[474] Manager John Cort and proprietor Will F. Fox opened the Tivoli Concert Hall on September 29 in the former Mechanic's Hotel on Main Street. John Cort, the most powerful theatre manager in the Pacific Northwest, may have planned to make the Tivoli a part of a chain of variety theatres in the region but the enterprise ran into legal problems. Arrests made at the concert hall resulted from letting women perform in an establishment that served liquor.[475] No further mention appeared in the press about shows at the Tivoli.

Four shows in October made it the liveliest entertainment month of the year. Haverly's Original Mastodon Minstrels pulled into town on October 1 with their usual entertaining array of artists.[476] In spite of the company title, Haverly did not feature pachyderms in his show. For some years minstrel companies had adopted such hyperbolic terms as "mastodon," "mammoth" and "spectacular" to describe their large casts and elaborate scenery. Three days after the minstrel, show Miss Grace McCrary, with the aid of local talent, presented an evening of elocution at the now seldom used Sonna Opera House.[477] On October 20 Robert Downing and Eugenie Blair starred in *The Gladiator* that drew a full house and led the press to label the performance as masterful.[478] Lincoln J. Carter, noted for his mounting of sensational melodramas, toured his production of *The Fast Mail* to Boise on October 29. The review noted that the "blood and thunder drama" did not require much from actors but that the character people "kept up" the comic portions of the play. But the large crowd came to see the "above average scenery" that included a climactic railway scene complete with a practical working engine, fourteen freight cars and an illuminated caboose. Lesser sensation scenes depicted "Niagara Falls at Midnight with Boiling Mist" and a realistic river scene with a steamboat explosion.[479]

Explosions of laughter greeted the Charles Frohman Company presentation of *Charley's Aunt* on November 5.[480] The local press wrote little about this still popular farce during its initial performance in Boise but had many more opportunities to review it as its revivals toured year after year. Boise's Knights of Pythias sponsored a local production of *Damon and Pythias* on November 23 with professional actors C. E. Sturges and Leonard G. Mitchell in the leading roles and local amateurs in support.[481] November's amusements ended on the twenty-ninth with Rusco and Smith's rendition of *Uncle Tom's Cabin*. Although the audience packed the Columbia Theatre, the *Statesman* condemned the entire company and viewed it "nothing short of a crime to disappoint such a magnificent house with a miserably poor presentation."[482]

Neil Burgess in *The County Fair* on December 6 helped relieve the disappointments over recent productions with a "splendid performance." In addition to good acting, *The County Fair* offered songs, dances and an exciting horse race scene during which three thoroughbred horses ran "three-quarters of a mile in full and continuous view of the audience."[483] Unfortunately, four days later Boise theatre patrons endured a rotten performance of *Jolly Old Chums* that elicited a scathing notice which compared it to the recent miserable showing of *Uncle Tom's Cabin*.[484] The month and year ended with "entertainment of high character" when the Calhoun Opera Company presented *Amorita*, the first of three shows, on December 31.[485]

1895

The downturn in the number of attractions performed in Boise reversed dramatically in 1895 as the public attended approximately sixty-six varied amusements that more than doubled the number of performances seen in 1894. Forty-five plays constituted most of the season with the rest of it consisting of operas and minstrel shows plus various concerts, circuses, medicine shows, magicians, impersonators and vaudeville.

The Calhoun Opera Company opened the 1895 season by completing a three day engagement begun on the final day of the previous year. Alice Beauvert, Frederick Huntley, Douglas Flint and Edward Webb headed a company of fifty that presented *The Black Hussar* and an encore performance of *Amorita* on January 1 and 2. The productions pleased audiences with a "wealth of scenery, beautiful costumes, striking stage effects, coupled with a splendid chorus and leading voices."[486]

After presentations of *The New Boy* by the Gustave Frohman Company on January 17 and a local production of *The Tramp* (written by and starring Idaho actor Leonard Mitchell) on the twenty-second, the renowned McKee Rankin performed on the nights of January 25 and 26.[487] Except for Rankin himself, very little in the opening performance of *The Canuck* pleased the public or the press. The company redeemed itself with a closing production of Rankin's most famous play, *The Danites*, that the press hailed as a decided improvement

McKee Rankin
NYPL: Billy Rose Collection
TH-45567

in which the "support did splendidly."[488] On January 28 Sadie Martinet and Max Figman earned praise for a successful presentation of *The Passport*.[489]

Longtime Boise favorite Katie Putnam played three nights and a matinee between January 31 and February 2. With her familiar repertory of *The Old Lime Kiln*, *The Little Maverick*, *Erma the Elf* and *The Old Curiosity Shop*, she delighted those in attendance with her "decidedly clever work" that "filled the theatre with sunshine one minute and the next with handkerchief[s] and tear-dimmed eyes." George Klint, Emery, Sadie Radcliffe, Gus Cohen and others supported Miss Putnam in winning the hearts of large audiences.[490] The local production of *The Dress Rehearsal* that followed the Putnam Company at the Columbia Theatre on February 14 and 16 also toured to Caldwell on February 19.[491]

Advance notices from Portland, Pendelton and Baker, Oregon papers reprinted in the *Statesman* raised local interest in the appearance of Charlotte, Essie and Minnie Tittell who enjoyed a regional reputation and were supported by Walter Monroe, Frederick Clark and other members of the W. S. Ford Company. Publicity emphasized Minnie Tittell's between acts specialty, a "serpentine dance" in which she wore a dress made of 125 yards of satin. Essie Tittell and Walter Monroe carried the emotional lines in the opening production of *Drifted Apart*; Minnie won the hearts of all in her portrayal of a blind girl and Charlotte as "the gay and vivacious creature of society" impressed the large audience with her talents. The sisters scored another hit with *Frou Frou* on February 19, but were less successful with *A Scrap of Paper* the following night which the press kindly blamed on the play rather than the performers. By special request the Tittell sisters and the Ford Company repeated *Frou Frou* as the closing show on February 20, but drew a smaller audience than the admirable performance deserved.[492]

Essie Tittell
University of Washington
Libraries Special Collections
PH Coll 59.533

Minnie Tittell
University of
Washington
Libraries Special
Collections
S-B-1277

Charlotte Tittell
University of Washington
Libraries Special
Collections
S-T-269

Immediately following the Tittell Sister's engagement, the Griffin-O'Neill Company arrived from Salt Lake City for shows on February 22 and 23. Performances by former leading lady Phosa McAllister, rising star Blanche Bates along with T. Daniel Frawley, Charles W. King, George Leslie and H.S. Duffield "captivated a large and critical audience."[493]

A disagreement between Manager Pinney and local ministers over the appearance of Tisso's "Living Pictures" on March 21 enlivened the local scene. Pinney assumed Tisso's living reproductions of some twenty famous paintings would be a "clean show." Ministers sought an injunction to prevent the show and objected to alleged nudity in the presentation. Pinney won no friends in the opposition when he pointed out that some local religious groups had sponsored living picture shows in their own churches. Tisso's Vaudeville, performed in spite of opposition, turned out to be a terrible entertainment. The paper blasted it as "exceedingly poor" with "drawn out specialty acts" accompanied by "many coarse and disgusting remarks and no end of horseplay." The reviewer found the controversial "living pictures" to be "poorly executed and a poor selection of subjects."[494]

Lord Rooney by the Pat Rooney Comedy Company on March 23, a concert by the local Verdi Society on April 18, the New York Specialty Company in vaudeville on April 20 and impersonations by Carrie Rudolph on April 24 preceded the appearances of Maude Granger's Company at the Columbia Theatre on May 7 and 8.[495] In *Camille* on opening night Maude Granger gave "one of the most satisfying performances in months." She made another hit the next evening in *The Fringe of Society*. John Maguire, owner of the Butte, Montana theatre, had joined with Maude Granger's Company, returning to Boise for the first time in nineteen years.[496]

Maude Granger
University of Washington Libraries Special Collections
PH Coll 75.274

In the *Statesman's* view, the cast of *The Girl I Left Behind Me*, presented by the Charles Frohman Company on May 14, lacked the strength of last year's company. The editor suggested that the "unnatural" love interest "formed the dry spots in the piece" and that "the Indian fighting would go much better in the east."[497] John Griffith received much kinder notices for his productions of *Faust* and *The Bells* on May 17 and 18. Griffith, who appeared annually in Idaho for several years, utilized a carload of scenery, ten calcium lights and a complete electrical plant in presenting Henry Irving's then popular version of *Faust*. Notices praised the spectacular effects, but felt Griffith relied on scenery and mechanical effects for his success and suffered from "inferior support" by his company. Griffith rose above his support in *The Bells* for a better received show on closing night.[498]

A medicine show by the O. K. T. (Oregon Kidney Tea) Company occupied the Sonna Opera House during the end of May and the first week in June. Manager Myers and a company of six to eight performers charged admission for variety entertainments such as serpentine dancing, Japanese juggling and short farces, all performed between spiels promoting a patent medicine. Although sales could not be made directly from the stage, business must have been good enough for Myers to extend the engagement through June 8.[499] The John B. Wills Company played opposite the medicine show on June 1, giving a creditable performance of *Two Old Cronies* at the Columbia Theatre.[500] Following the departure of the O. K. T. troupe, Eliason, the magician, arrived on June 10 to thrill audiences with two evenings of "marvels, miracles and magic" in a presentation entitled *After the Ball*.[501] June's amusements ended with performances of *A Woman's Bitter Atonement* and *Tom Roark's Vision*, "new and special plays" by the Webber Dramatic Company, on June 13 and 14. Webber cancelled a scheduled third performance because of disappointing ticket sales.[502]

Two circuses supplied the only amusements for July of 1895, an unidentified troupe on July 1 that stopped on its way to Payette and the Wallace Circus on July 26. The latter company attracted 5,000 patrons for each of two performances with some 1,000 of that number from out of town.[503] Lloyd's Big Pavilion Company presented *Uncle Tom's Cabin* on August 9 as the single amusement for the month. The "Tom Show" drew a good crowd into its "monster canvas opera house set up at the corner of 8th and Wall Street."[504]

William Gillette
University of Washington
Libraries Special Collections
PH Coll 59.228

September of 1895 began with an appearance of William Gillette, an eminent author and comedian famous for his creation of the role of Sherlock Holmes, as the star of Charles Frohman's production of *Too Much Johnson*. The show, given at the Columbia on September 14, allegedly featured exactly the same cast that played the comedy for 350 nights on Broadway.[505]

Over a week later, on September 23, the Pringle and May Company began the longest single engagement of the year when it opened at the Columbia Theatre in *Miss Nobody*. During the troupe's run of six evenings and a matinee it gave "universal satisfaction" in delightful performances that provoked "continual laughter." Press items described Johnny Pringle as a "born comedian" with a "creditable manner" and Edna May as a "very clever and charming little soubrette." In addition to acting

Edna May
NYPL: Billy Rose
Collection Th-34430

Miss May made a hit with her striking "Kaleidoscopic Dance," performed between acts of plays. Dressed in 100 yards of silk, she danced before and among screens illuminated by calcium lights that changed the color and appearance of her dress 100 times in ten minutes. Her movements suggested "the various forms of butterflies, spiders, fowls and fishes." Pringle and May possessed most of the talent in the troupe and received weak support from their less gifted hirelings. In addition to their opening show, Pringle and May presented *Eccles Girl, Married in Haste, My Sweetheart, Little Nell* and *East Lynne* during their season.[506] The lives of Pringle and May held interest beyond their Idaho appearances. During the summer of 1895, on July 10, Pringle's wife in Logan, Utah gave birth to a son who was to become silent film star John Gilbert. Miss May went on to become a star in New York and London who later married a New York millionaire.

As the first of three entertainments in October, one hundred Boiseans participated in the pantomime production of *The Magic Doll* on the tenth to raise money for the synagogue fund of the Beth Israel congregation.[507] Two railroad melodramas, *The Pay Train* on the twelfth and a repeat showing of Lincoln J. Carter's *The Fast Mail* on October 31, rounded out the entertainment offerings for the month.[508]

A crowded house called "Peerless" Pauline Hall before the Columbia Theatre curtain for many encores after her performance in the opera *Dorcas* on November 8.[509] Three days later Charlotte Tittell returned to the Boise stage, this time with out her sisters, to star in *A Woman of the World* and *Gloriana*. Miss Tittell "required little ability to portray the lead character" and, except for a Mr. Munro, had weak support. Indisposed for the second show, the unfortunate actress fainted in the last act, but recovered sufficiently to perform in Caldwell the following evening.[510] Mahara's Refined Minstrels, headed by Billie Young and Hilland Brewer, had only a fair house on

November 13 for a performance marred by undistinguished olio acts and bad singing that offered "more noise than harmony."[511]   On November 14 Lincoln J. Carter once again excited a crowded house with his melodrama, *Tornado* that, although a literary failure, triumphed as a scenic production. The thriller's scenes included the dissecting room of a medical college and a climactic "rigging scene" with six sailors furling a monster sail as two ocean liners collided in "mountain high" waves.[512] Charlotte Tittell returned to the Columbia stage on November 28 for the third time in 1895 to fill a date cancelled by Katie Emmett. A triple bill of plays (*Sweethearts, My Uncle Will, International Match*) attracted only a fair house.[513] After this performance Charlotte Tittell and some company members remained in Boise. On December 4 Wallace Monroe and Miss Tittell advertised their willingness to "accept pupils for elocution and practical stage training" and Monroe became the stage manager for a James Pinney benefit scheduled for December 5. Their stay in Boise ended on December 10 when they announced their acceptance of twenty-one weeks of work in Salt Lake City.[514]

Schilling's Minstrels commenced December's entertainments with a performance on the third that featured six comedians in a "Grand Shakespearean First Part" which failed to please a crowded house and a second part that pleased immensely.[515] In spite of rainy weather on December 5, Pinney's benefit attracted a large crowd that enjoyed the talents of Charlotte Tittlell, local lawyer William Borah and others.[516] Amateur and professional theatre productions closed out the theatrical season of 1895. Local talent under the direction of Mrs. Hinges presented *Temple of Fame* on December 9 and the Charles Frohman touring version of *Charley's Aunt* paid a return visit to the capital city on December 12 to be well received by a good house.[517]

1896

For no apparent reason the number of shows presented in the 1896 entertainment year dropped almost twenty-five percent as only forty-five performances played in Boise during the year. Again plays prevailed as the major means of diversion, followed by a smattering of opera, minstrels, etc. The only slight deviation from the usual pattern of attractions derived from a successful engagement of Professor Bristol's "Eques Curriculum," an exhibition featuring several trained horses.

January set a rapid pace for theatricals with no less than a dozen performances during the month, eleven by three professional troupes and a single amateur production. Eunice Goodrich and her company occupied the rarely used stage of the Sonna Opera House for the week of January sixth. The Sonna theatrical operation had been taken over by Spaulding and Gordon a few weeks earlier and engaged Miss Goodrich as the first of several quality attractions promised by the new proprietors.[518] Except for a few performers, Eunice Goodrich did have a solid company, including Dave Rivers and the cute Pottle's Baby—a five-year old child—in specialties. They managed to have a successful week of business presenting such works as *Sweet Briar, M'lss, Little Miss Worth, Wanted, a Husband, The Banker's Daughter, Fun in a Boarding School* and *Little Romp.* Although she won praise for her own acting and the quality of her productions, her most welcome innovation—a thirty-cent admission price—pleased the most of all.[519]

Eunice Goodrich
University of
Washington Libraries
Special Collections
PH Coll 5-8-336

Katie Putnam made another one of her frequent visits to Boise to entertain at the Columbia Theatre on January 14 and 15 in a familiar dramatic vehicle, *The Old Lime Kiln*. According to advertising placed by her advance agent, W. O. Wheeler, the cottage and grounds of Miss Putnam's summer home in Benton Harbor, Michigan served as a model for one set in the show. Of more interest to Boise's public was the presence of Leonard G. Mitchell, a former Lewiston and Boise resident, in the Putnam Company. A large crowd, undaunted by stormy weather, greeted him with a "rousing ovation" upon his first entrance in his role of Bud Markley. Notices the following day found Mitchell's "character work exceptionally good." Miss Putnam earned her usual plaudits as the "same winsome Katie" who stands "head and shoulders above all the soubrettes that have appeared in Boise." Others mentioned in the review were E. L. Lee, H. B. Emery, J. Rentfrow, Eva Thatcher and Tom Findley. After an equally successful second performance, the Putnam Company and Leonard Mitchell went on to Caldwell.[520]

A presentation of Lincoln J. Carter's *The Defaulter* interrupted January's run of successful, quality shows when it unfolded before a disappointed Boise audience on January 17 at the Columbia. Although Carter shows had thrilled in the past, this melodrama could not hide bad acting with beautiful scenery and spectacular effects. The play depended on a climactic scene that called for the hero and heroine, mounted on horseback, to make a double "leap for life" over an abyss! For the effect stuffed dummy replicas of horses and riders attached to a large pendulum-like beam swung out over the stage to complete the seemingly death-defying leap. The audience saw right through the clumsy effect and, as the *Statesman* reviewer wrote, it was the "horse that got the horse laugh."[521]

Under the auspices of the Sherman House a group of local talents presented *A Proposal Under Difficulties* on January 29.[522] Burt Hodgkins and company closed out the busy month on January 30 with a performance of *Uncle Josh Spruceby*. Supposedly an entertaining "hick" comedy, advertising for the show emphasized a realistic sawmill scene complete with a thirty-six inch steel blade and notices stated that the best scene depicted a girl being fed into the over-sized saw. Presumably, as in other sawmill scenes, the girl escaped becoming so much lumber. With more specialties than plot, the show gained most of its entertainment value from a good orchestra and a "hayseed" band.[523]

Theatrical activity dropped off appreciably in February with the Columbia Theatre open for only four nights. As a benefit for the Free Reading Room, the Columbian Club sponsored *The Breach of Promise Case* on February 3, a local effort that included future United States Senator William E. Borah among its participants.[524] On February 5 and 6, Effie Essler, noted for creating the title role of *Hazel Kirke* on Broadway, performed in *As You Like It* and *Camille* with her father, John Essler, in support along with Frank Weston and Holbrook Blinn. Her productions played to full houses and gained favorable review for her and the supporting players.[525] The only other show of the month, Bowman and Young's Minstrels on February 25, had a good house.[526]

During the month of March performers continued to appear infrequently with only two companies engaged for the month. "Prince Roy" and "Little Virginia," juvenile performers with the J. P. Howe Company, won the hearts of the audience in a production of *The American Girl* on March 16 at the Columbia. Light attendance at *From Florida to Mexico* the next evening resulted from the Boise public looking forward to the Tavary Opera engagement a week later. As a *Statesman* reporter explained, "people consulted their purses" and decided to save up for the opera.[527] Tickets for Marie Tavary's Grand Opera

Marie Tavary
State Library
of Victoria
Australia H 9124

Company cost from one to two and a half dollars, a sizable increase in price, but this did not deter Boiseans from filling the Columbia for three opera performances between March 23 and 24. Light opera companies had played Boise on occasion in the past, but the Tavary troupe became the first grand opera company to ever play in the capital city. Even though the singers had to ride for thirty-six hours to get to Boise, they overcame understandable fatigue and gave a performance that delighted a "large and fashionable audience." Local press notices enthusiastically praised and complimented the singers as well as the orchestra, the "best ever in Boise." On opening night the company presented a double bill of *Lucia di Lammermoor* and *Cavalleria Rusticana* followed the next day by a matinee performance of *Faust* and an evening offering of *Carmen* to close a most successful season.[528]

Amusement became ever scarcer in April when the Boise public had only three entertainments to attend. Murray and Mack, popular west coast comedians, starred in a farce, *Finnegan's Ball*, on April 11. Leopold Godowsky, renowned concert pianist gave a recital on April 13 at the Columbia before a disappointingly small audience. The paper scolded the public for not attending and for missing out on an opportunity to hear great music. A local female minstrel show on April 16 appealed more to the public's taste as patrons packed the Columbia to see the local lasses.[529]

May, too, offered only three occasions for people to attend the theatre. On May 13 and 14 John Griffith paid a return visit to Boise with productions of *Faust* and *The Fool's Revenge*. The press duly noted that Griffith, the youngest actor then playing the role of Mephisto, brought to the part a highly original interpretation. Notices also detected an improvement in Griffith's supporting cast that last year "was not what it should have been." Miss Curtis as Marguerite won praise as did the production's special effects that included an "electrical duel," "a shower of fire" and "curling sulphurous smoke." Griffith ended the brief season with a splendid rendering of *The Fool's Revenge*.[530] As the final May entertainment elocutionist Arthur Redwood also gained extravagant press commentary for his presentation of *Stray Leaves* at the Sonna Opera House on May 16.[531] Then, from mid-May to early September, the only entertainment group to perform in Boise was a circus presented by the Great Wallace Shows on June 22.[532]

Theatre business picked up significantly in September with a total of ten evenings of entertainment. Professor Bristol's Trained Horses—advertised as "Eques Curriculum"—opened the September season on the third and played through the fifth. About two weeks later, on September 17, Edouard Remenyi enraptured Boiseans with his skill as a violinist. On September 21 Miss Orris Ober and her company of fifteen eastern artists began a week long season at the Columbia Theatre in a production of *Myrtle Ferns*. After playing a week with some success, the company extended its run through September 29, appearing in such plays as *Mixed Pickles*, *For a Million*, *Trilby* and *The Bells*.[533]

Only three shows went before the footlights in October and the audience might well have wished the number one less. Miss Lillian Keene and company in *The Bowery Girl* on October 3 "bilked" a large crowd with "one of the worst of the long list of fakes inflicted on a long suffering theatre-going public." A candid review accused "wretched" singers of murdering songs, but described the dancing as "fairly good."[534] Gus Heege, better known as the Swedish character Yon Yonson, fared much better before a full house for his presentation of *A Yenuine Yentleman* on October 5.[535] So did the famous bridge jumper, Steve Brodie, when he starred in *On the Bowery* on October 19, a play that, to no surprise, featured a jump from the Brooklyn Bridge as its sensation scene.[536]

The remainder of October and all of November passed without record of a single theatrical event. Two local events occupied the Columbia stage in December: *David*, a cantata on December 7 and *The Hidden Hand* by the Boise Stock Dramatic Company on the following evening. According to its reviewer, the latter production deserved a better house than it attracted.[537]

1897

The number of entertainments presented in the 1897 season increased significantly to seventy three. Legitimate drama in all its various forms continued to provide the most engagements with five companies playing seasons ranging from three to ten evenings. Until September touring stock companies gave most of the performances, but after that traveling combinations provided the majority of shows. Other entertainments appeared for only one or two evenings at a time with the exception of a hypnotist and a magician who both played week long engagements.

Theatre companies offered Boise audiences both spectacular melodramas and classical drama during limited January and February seasons. The Cook Twin Sisters brought their $20,000 production of *Uncle Tom's Cabin* direct from Portland to Boise on January 7. The company advertised a cast of forty people, a military band and twenty ponies along with "Man Eating Siberian Blood Hounds" headed by Ajax, "the $5,000 Champion Beauty." This troupe's Eva traveled in a $3,000 golden chariot, while Uncle Tom got along with a "typical southern ox-cart."[538] A much less costly production of *The Black Flag* by the Boise Stock Amateur Club on January 11 starred Frank Paine who received fair support from local talent.[539] Renowned Shakespearean actor Louis James—supported by Guy Lindsley, Miss Kreuger and Miss Everett—gave great satisfaction with a short season of classical dramas at the Columbia on January 22 and 23. Large audiences filled the theatre to witness evening performances of *Spartacus* and *Othello* and a matinee showing of *Romeo and Juliet*.[540] An amateur group under the management of C. E. Cole gave the only

February performance when it joined with the Sheridan Drum Corps to present *Nugget Nell* at the Sonna Opera House on the twenty-fourth.[541]

Amusement opportunities increased tenfold in March beginning with Ferguson and Emerick's combination, *McSorley's Twins*, at the Columbia on March 3.[542] The Grover Company played two evenings and a matinee between March 5 and 6. Leonard Grover, Jr. and May Noble in the opening night double bill of *Everybody's Friend* and *The Open Gate* gained the admiration of the local reviewer even though, in his opinion, some of their support did not come up to "requirements." He found the play good as a whole and "devoid of the horse-play with which Boise theatre-goers have been surfeited." The twelve member company presented *Cad, the Tomboy* and *The Wolves of New York* at matinee and evening performances on March 6.[543] Over two weeks later, on March 24 and 25, George Riddle gave readings at the Methodist Church.[544] A few days later Eunice Goodrich returned to perform on the Sonna Opera House stage in *Captain January* and *My Wife*. These March 29 and 30 performances offered additional entertainment in the form of the "Viarescope," the latest and best picture machine, that projected railroad scenes of the Empire State Express.[545] Professor Gunning, appearing at the Columbia Theatre in competition with the Goodrich company, employed another picture machine, the "Vitoscope," to augment his hypnotism exhibitions scheduled for March 29 through April 3.[546] Within a decade these short motion picture novelties, often utilized only to fill time between acts, would transform the entertainment world and forever alter the theatre industry in America.

Two substantial engagements by traveling stock companies gave Boise theatre patrons a choice to attend more than a dozen shows in April. Senter Payton's Big Comedy Company with its "Challenge Band and full operatic orchestra" opened a week long season on April 12 with *The Black Flag*. During the rest of the engagement the company, which included Senter Payton, Miss Lucy, Miss Vina, Curtis, Fred Moore, Del Forrest and the Payton sisters, produced such works as *The Octoroon, A Yankee in Cuba* and *Uncle Josh Whitcomb.*[547] Before the next professional company arrived in town, local amateurs presented *Betsy Baker*, a one-act farce, at the G.A.R. Hall on April 21.[548] Originally scheduled for April 19, the engagement of the Hettie Bernard Chase Company began four days later due to a railroad washout near Huntington, Oregon that delayed them after completing a season in Baker, Oregon. The train finally got through and the troupe opened on April 23 in *Little Coquette*, the beginning of a ten day run—the longest in many years. Thirty cent tickets and satisfactory productions attracted substantial audiences during the season. At one point in the run, the troupe initiated the unusual practice of introducing specialties between the acts of the old tragedy, *Damon and Pythias*, with the result that Miss Pyne's rendering of a character song convulsed the audience with laughter. For the production of *Under Two Flags*, the troupe enlisted soldiers from the military post to swell the ranks on stage. Company members listed in print during the season were Master Charlie Chase, Miss Pyne, George Hayes, Chase, Herne, Mrs. Herne, Henderson, Kennie, McLeod, and Walter Brooks. *Uncle's Darling* and *Kathleen Mavourneen*, presented at matinee and evening performances on May 1, concluded the Chase Company's successful Boise stay at the Columbia Theatre.[549]

Theatre activity in early May began actively enough, but tailed off at mid-month. Russ Whytal's *In Fair Virginia* aggregation played to a good house only three days after the Chase troupe closed.[550] Georgia Cayvan and her troupe immediately succeeded Whytal at the Columbia on May 5 and 6 with presentations of *Mary Pennington, Spinster* and *Squire Kate*. The opening show had to do without its special scenery due to a late train, but the second show went up "exactly as presented in New York." Both shows attracted large audiences and elicited compliments for Miss Cayvan's talents, a strong supporting company and all round splendid presentation.[551]   A week passed after the Cayvan troupe left for Pocatello and then the Grover Company that had played Boise in March returned to present the last shows of the month in a repeat performance of *Cad, the Tomboy* on May 14 and a new production, *Ranch 10*, on May 15.[552]

Georgia Cayvan
University of
Washington Libraries
Special Collections
PH Coll 59.91

June had nothing to offer in the way of entertainment except performances by the Walter L. Main Circus on June 22.[553] July was nearly over before the Simpson and Edwards Stock Company, fresh from the Maguire Opera House in Butte, Montana, came to town to commence a week's engagement on July 26 at the Columbia Theatre. Vitascope motion pictures of "The Great Corbett Fight" helped fill intermissions in the troupe's productions of such old standards as *The Ticket-Of-Leave Man* and *The Streets of New York*. A repeat showing of *Tit for Tat*, presented earlier in the run, ended the engagement on July 31.[554]

Theatres stayed closed during August and for the first two weeks of September. Finally, a combination company came to Boise on September 16 and 17 to present *Si Perkins* and *Our Old Kentucky Home*.[555] The only other show of the month, an amateur production of *Fogg's Ferry* directed by Mr. Hoffstadt for the Boise Histrionic Society, attracted a small but appreciative audience at the Columbia on September 28.[556]

October proved to be as meager a month for amusements as the previous one. Eliason Dante returned with his magic show to play the week of October 11 at the Columbia.[557] Exciting melodrama attracted good houses on October 22 and 23 for yet another Lincoln J. Carter thriller, *The Hearts of Chicago*. According to the *Statesman* review, nothing presented in Boise before compared with the mechanical stage effects utilized in the climactic scene of the melodrama, a ten-minute railroad scene in which "an attempt is made to wreck an oncoming train by plunging it into the river through an open draw [bridge]." The effect called for the train to appear as a speck of light in the distance and then approach the audience growing larger and louder until "finally the train dashes panting under a full head of steam down to the footlights." Fortunately for the Boiseans in the orchestra section, the train stopped at the footlights "within a few feet of the brave girl who has turned to view the red light signal of danger to save her lover." As if this were not excitement enough, another scene in the play recreated the famous Chicago fire complete with fire engines, falling walls, flying timbers and leaping flames.[558] The following attraction, *Sam'l of Posen* with M. B. Curtis on October 30, relied on character comedy rather than spectacular scenes to attract and entertain its audience. Curtis had played his "impersonation of Hebrew character" for eighteen years. He had reportedly earned a million dollars in that time. Although the production served mainly as a vehicle for Curtis, the press made special mention of the clever artists in his strong supporting cast.[559]

Cosgrove and Grant's *The Dazzler* got November's theatre activities off to a rousing start at the Columbia on the third where an immense audience delighted in the "vim and snap" of the show's songs and dances performed by a troupe of comics and comely chorus girls.[560] Louis James brought entertainment of a more legitimate nature to Boise with his productions on November 8 and 9. The press regarded the company's opening production, *A Cavalier of France*, as a poor vehicle for an actor of James' deserved reputation. A strong supporting cast merited praise except for a Miss Hendricks "who gave the audience the horrors—she cannot act and her attempts were simply painful." James and company did much better the next day and evening in "highly satisfactory" presentations of *Spartacus* and *Julius Caesar* before well filled houses.[561] Ten days later Digby Bell and his supporting company of twenty-three staged *The Hoosier Doctor* at the Columbia and were followed the next evening, November 20, by a poorly attended melodrama, James Walters' production of *Side Tracked.*[562] Later in the week, on November 26 and 27, twenty-eight year old John Griffith again played before large Boise audiences in critically acclaimed presentations of *Faust* and *Richard III.*[563]

Almost three weeks passed in December before the first entertainment arrived in Boise. For fifty cents the Edward Shields Company, booked at the Columbia on December 20, promised an evening of specialties, illustrated songs and "To Klondike and Return," a motion picture shown by the Edison Projectoscope. During the Shields' performance some of the Columbia Theatre's floor joists caught on fire, causing slight damage, but not affecting the show or the audience. Lack of heat in the theatre that night when the temperature dropped to fourteen above zero led a *Statesman* reporter to write: "the audience did not know there was a fire in the vicinity of the theatre and if they had known it they probably would have hovered about the flames instead of becoming panic stricken."[564]

Katie Putnam, who had performed in Boise at various times over at least the last twelve years, returned once more on December 22 in a production of *Tom Tinker's Kid.* Idaho actor Leonard Mitchell remained in her troupe, but his appearance in an unimportant role disappointed his Boise friends.[565] At the Methodist Church on the evening of the Putnam performance, Lottie Tillotson held forth in an evening of elocutionary entertainment.[566] On Christmas Day the Francis Jones combination presented *In Old Madrid* at the Columbia.[567] At the same theatre on December 29, Harry Martell's *South Before the War*, a combination of *Uncle Tom's Cabin* and a minstrel show, drew an immense crowd including Nampa residents who came to Boise by means of a special excursion train for the event. No doubt advertisements describing the "Piccaniny Band," the "Landing of the Robert E. Lee," a "Cotton Picking scene," "Pastimes on the Levee," and a "Great Cake Walk" helped lure patrons to the Columbia. While the show disappointed some, the paper judged it good in its entirety with special commendation to its skilled acrobats.[568] A concert by St. Theresa's Academy bought the 1897 entertainment season to an end.[569]

1898

As theatre business expanded and improved generally on the west coast and in the Pacific Northwest during 1898, more and more traveling combination productions that traveled the rail route to major centers such as Portland and Seattle stopped to perform in Boise and Pocatello. While Boise drew its share of the combination shows, its growing population and the presence of the spacious and well-equipped Columbia Theatre also attracted traveling stock companies that played profitable seasons of a week or more. Between the combinations and the stock companies, Boise audiences did not lack for diversion as they occupied seats at the Columbia Theatre and the Sonna Opera House over ninety times in 1898.

Season opener *The Pulse of New York* on January 7 and 8 drew a large house for its first performance, but failed to attract a like patronage for the repeat showing.[570] A "rainbow dance" and thirteen other big specialties plus the talents of comedians Ned Monroe and Billy Hart lured a large house to the Columbia Theatre for *The Gay Matinee Girl* on January 26. Only some unwarranted "horse play" marred an otherwise entertaining show.[571]

Jules Grau's Opera Company played the first of what were to be many Boise engagements during the week of February 7. The talents of the forty member company and a reasonable seventy-five cent admission assured well filled houses throughout the run. Offer of additional savings through purchase of a season ticket precipitated a heavy advance sale for the opera season. *La Mascotte*, the opening selection, pleased the audience with its "local hits" (specially added allusions to Boise people, places or events) and a high-kicking tambourine dance.[572] *Fra Diavolo*, presented on February 8, overshadowed the opening show in terms of music and drama, but had too little comedy and too much opera to please the local tastes.[573] Little press commentary followed presentations of *Girofle-Girofla* and *Boccaccio* at matinee and evening performances on Wednesday that filled the Columbia Theatre to the doors. The *Statesman* criticized the February 10 presentation of *Ship Ahoy* as too light a work and not up to the previous standards of Grau's performers. The press also found fault with the rendering of *Bohemian Girl* on February 11, particularly the abilities of some singers, but applauded the performance as pleasing overall. At the end of the opera actors came before the curtain to thank the packed house for its patronage and to announce the company's intentions to return next year. A matinee performance of *The Chimes of Normandy* and an evening presentation of *Olivette* on Saturday, February 12 ended an opera season which had been so popular that it had curtailed society events in Boise for the week.[574]

    Under the Dome, still another Lincoln J. Carter sensation drama, featured elaborate scenic effects in its presentation at the Columbia Theatre on March 4. A hurricane scene and a ferryboat ride from Jersey City to New York, "said to be marvelously like the real thing," attracted a fair crowd that enjoyed the effects so much that "many of them were repeated several times at the request of the audience."[575] The Empire Comedy Company opened an engagement of two weeks at the seldom used Sonna Opera House (now managed by J. W. Blake) on March 7. A ten, twenty, thirty cent troupe, the Empire Comedy company drew fair-sized to large audiences until near the end of its season with productions from a rather standard repertoire plus a few newer plays.[576] The company had only one rival show during its season, a poorly received appearance of the Georgia Operatic Minstrels at the Columbia on March 14.[577]

Days before the Empire Comedy Company closed out its performances on March 19 and left for Mountain Home, advance agent M. B. "Goldie" Goldstein of the renowned Bittner Company arrived in Boise to make arrangements to open a one-week season at the Columbia on March 21. Bittner's traveling stock company, highly recommended in eastern press exchanges, charged fifty cents for its show and used an Edison Triograph projector for motion pictures between scenes. Members of the company included W. W. Bittner, John Waldron, Edward Kelly, Mattie Choate, Millie Stevens, Walter Fredericks, McClellan and Moran. Liberal applause for the opening night attraction of *Friends* "broadened into a rattling curtain call" for almost every member of the company. The next day, notices hailed the Bittner Company as the best popular priced company ever in Boise. Business for subsequent performances remained so good that Bittner extended the run for two days. Although Bittner presented such old favorites as *Rip Van Winkle* and *Davey Crockett*, his repertoire included some recent high royalty shows like *Charley's Aunt*. Bittner and troupe went on to Baker, Oregon after a final Boise appearance on March 29.[578]

While stock companies had provided most of the entertainment in March, combination troupes offered the Boise public a variety of shows and performers in April. Noted Irish character actor Daniel Sully did not fare well in attracting audiences for his productions of *O'Brien the Contractor* and *Auld Lang Syne* at the Columbia on April 8 and 9

Daniel Sully
University of
Washington
Libraries
Special
Collections
S-831

even though reviews declared his productions and his support to be "of first order."[579] In contrast, a good house attended the Columbia on April 13 to enjoy Charles E. Blaney's *A Boy Wanted* that promised, and delivered, "Farce, Burlesque, Comedy, Vaudeville, Extravaganza, All In One."[580]

James O'Neill
Joseph Harworth
Collection
www.josephharworth.com

James O'Neill, father of playwright Eugene O'Neill and one of the most famous actors of his day, appeared at the Columbia on April 14 in his most distinguished role, *Monte Cristo*, a part he had performed over 3,000 times. While advance performance publicity emphasized the play's "Carload of Scenery" and "A Chaos of Calcium Effects," O'Neill's reputation was instrumental in attracting a sizable house. He and his excellent company gave a finished performance that had "little to criticize and much to praise." Notices cited O'Neill as a polished actor possessed of a "masterful manner."[581] Frederick Warde, another nationally acclaimed actor, starred in his company's presentations of *Virginius* and *Ingomar* on April 20 and 21. In addition to the evening productions, Warde delivered a lecture on Shakespeare during the afternoon of the second show. Although his display of histrionic powers impressed a large audience on opening night, a press item expressed the need for Warde to overcome the rather outdated script of *Virginius*—a play dating back to 1820. *Ingomar* on the final evening appealed to a fair-sized audience.[582] Janet Waldorf and her company "of much merit," playing *Ingomar* again just five nights later, understandably gained only a small audience, but Miss Waldorf won press recognition as "a brilliant star" in the role of Parthenia. She gave another first class performance in *The Hunchback* on April 28.[583]

May's amusements began with a series of combination shows and ended with a week of stock theatre. Another Charles E. Blaney production began the month's entertainments with Thomas J. Ryan and twenty pretty girls in *The Hired Girl*. The press dismissed the show as the "ordinary vaudeville kind such as infest beer halls but is seldom admitted into respectable theatres."[584] Thearle's Nashville Students followed on May 5 and 6 with a concert at the Methodist Church.[585] Notices described the presentation of *Miss Frances of Yale* by the Brenton Thorpe Company on May 6 as "funnier than *Charley's Aunt*." The farce starred Etienne Giradot, supposedly the "only original 'Charley's Aunt.'"[586] The next evening's performance of *Old Innocence* with Tim Murphy gained a fair house and an equally fair review.[587] May's entertainment events ended with six performances by the Jossey-Marvin stock company that featured Mr. Jossey and Miss Howard. Popular admission prices and a solid supporting company kept the Columbia Theatre auditorium filled from the opening production of *Under Two Flags* on May 16 to the concluding performance of *The Volunteer* on May 21.[588]

Few performers stopped in Boise from June through August of 1898 and nobody came in September at all. The Somers Family performers that entertained on June 8 and 9 at the Columbia Theatre deserved better patronage than they received.[589] Lecturer, humorist Robert Burdett suffered from a similar lack of attendance for his appearance of June 11 on the same stage.[590] Performances on July 1 and 2 by Rose Melville in a farce-comedy, *The Prodigal Father*, attracted fair size audiences who laughed, yelled and enjoyed "fun in the form of specialties."[591] On August 6 the Norris Brothers set up a tent at Eighth and Bannock for a performance of their dog and pony show.[592]

Unusual events marked a rather busy October entertainment calendar. Soprano Geneva Jennings' concert on October 2 attracted a large audience, unusual at the time for the Boise public. The appearance of Held's Military Band, a popular local organization, may have helped swell the attendance.[593] Also unusual was the simultaneous week long engagements of two reputable stock companies at rival Boise theatres, a situation that would become more common in later years. As part of the attractions for Fair Week, the Bittner Company, that had played earlier in May, returned to begin the first of six performances on October 2 with *The Galley Slave* at the Columbia Theatre. On the same date the Noble Dramatic Company opened an identical six show run in *The Strategist* at the Sonna Opera House.[594] During the week both companies offered popular priced shows and both seemed to have prospered with the press indicating full or large houses each evening at the two theatres.[595] Yet another unusual amusement event occurred during the week of October 18 at the Sonna Opera House when Professor Edward Mozart, comedy illusionist, and May Kennedy, singing comedienne, presented Edison's Original Moving Picture and Specialty Company. Although motion pictures had been shown as part of entertainments for several years in Boise, here for the first time the pictures made up the major part of the evening's entertainment.[596] October's unusual theatrical occurrences came to an end with productions of two Lincoln J. Carter shows, repeat engagements of *The Heart of Chicago* on October 20 and *Under the Dome* a week later. At the performance of *Under the Dome* the "audience cheered itself hoarse at this marvel of stage mechanics," ignoring the inadequacies of the leading man that the press described as "stiff as a poker and about as undramatic." The same critic expressed gratitude for the unnamed leading lady who "seemed to appreciate the fact that something besides scene shifting was necessary to make a successful performance.[597]

On November 3 Boise theatre-goers endured more "scene shifting" in *The Airship*, a musical farce with the original New York cast. The show introduced an airship in the second act that carried fifteen passengers across the stage. Unfortunately the large audience had to sit through a "great deal of very cheap horse play" before seeing the evening's novel mechanical effect.[598] The Women's Auxiliary of the Episcopal Church presented *An Oriental Fete* on November 15 and 16 at the Columbia, an effort that involved sixty-five Boise residents.[599] On November 26 Mahara's Mammoth Minstrels filled the Columbia stage with variety entertainers.[600]

Chattanooga, another of Lincoln J. Carter's seemingly inexhaustible series of melodramas, opened the final month of 1898 amusements. As usual for a Carter show, the play depended on a climactic scenic effect, supplied in this play by the utilization of a stationary railroad engine and the projection of moving pictures on a rear screen that gave the illusion that the engine was flying along at sixty miles an hour as hero and villain fought fiercely in a hand-to-hand combat. Unfortunately during the Boise presentation, the electrical system failed, making it impossible to use the motion picture scenery. Understandably, "the fight had much of the sensation knocked out of it."[601]

Hi Henry's All White Minstrels filled an engagement at the Columbia on December 8 and 9, the fifty member company appearing as "jolly jackies (sailors) aboard the cruiser Brooklyn."[602] Although condemned by devotees of the old minstrel show form, groups such as Hi Henry's Minstrels resorted to ever more fanciful, often exotic, scenery and costumes in their productions. Roof gardens, Asian locales and even the court of Louis XIV replaced the folksy plantation scenes of earlier minstrelsy. The show that had opened the year, *The Pulse of New York*, returned to play the Columbia immediately after Hi Henry. Star Emyline Barr and specialty performers delighted with "an olio of fun."[603] On December 15 William Cader and company thrilled the audience in *The Span of Life*. In the only scene "worth staying up to see," the heroine and her child, fleeing from the pursuit of Arab white slavers, are trapped at the edge of a rocky gorge in Africa. All seems lost when an acrobatic troupe appears at the far side of the chasm, sees her plight, mounts into a three or four high shoulder stand, falls across the gorge, catches the other side and forms a living bridge that the heroine runs across to safety. Small wonder notices described the scene as "one of the most thrilling things seen here in a long time."[604]

Cosgrove and Grant's *The Dazzler* again played Boise on December 16 and 17, slightly more than a year after its last local performance. Now in its ninth year, its many features—including scenes in New York, London and France—made a hit with large audiences on both nights of presentation.[605] The 1898 theatre season ended with the Bittner Theatre Company's third engagement of the year at the Columbia Theatre. Between December 26 and 31 Bittner's group played six evenings and two matinees before substantial patronage. Newspaper accounts listed the fifteen members of the troupe: Mr. and Mrs. W. W. Bittner, Mr. and Mrs. Edward Kelley, Mr. and Mrs. Ned Mitchell, Mattie Choate, Milly Stevens, Mazeppa Kelly, John Waldron, Walter Fredericks, Lew Rose, Len McClellan, Chris Moran and Sam Driesbach. Cold weather and a sometimes inadequately heated theatre did not prevent audiences from attending a season of new plays and old favorites. A December 30 presentation of the familiar *East Lynne* merited extravagant praise for Bittner as the villain and for Miss Choate who "several times . . . caused the theatre to be dotted with handkerchiefs held to tear dimmed eyes." Tears gave way to laughter as the Bittner Company closed its season on December 31 with a farce, *The Pug Dog and the Baby.*[606]

1899

The ninety some entertainments offered to Boise audiences in 1899 maintained the same level of amusement activity as in the previous year. While the number of play productions dropped to about fifty, dramatic fare still remained the major form of entertainment. Performances of operas, minstrel shows and concerts along with motion picture exhibitions and demonstrations of hypnotism increased slightly for the year while such diversions as circuses and equestrian shows appeared for only one or two presentations.

During an eventful January season, the Columbia Theatre hosted eleven performances. *Alone in Greater New York*, on January 4, mixed sentiment and sensation to entertain its audience. Star Dorothy Lewis made a hit with her portrayal of a tiny waif and an exploding

Dorothy Morton
University of
Washington
Libraries Special
Collections S-M-114

warehouse effect supplied thrilling spectacle.[607] *On the Suwanee*, presented January 9, featured Stella Mahew and, as a souvenir of the production's two hundredth performance, the show's producers offered a hundred beautiful song sheets to ladies in attendance.[608] Stormy weather during the following evening failed to keep away a large crowd for the performance of *Girofle-Girofla* by the Dorothy Morton Opera Company, the opening night of a three show run. Supported by thirty-five "carefully trained voices," Miss Morton carried the show and gave the audience "unbounded" pleasure. Matinee and evening performances of *Fra Diavolo* and *The Beggar Student* on January 11 met with similar success.[609] Performances of the melodramatic *Shaft No. 2* on January 20 and 21 earned hearty applause for a good company in a strong play with the best electrical display seen in a long time.[610]

On January 23 and 24 John Lindsay and his company returned to Boise after an absence of ten years to present his old standbys, *Ingomar* and *Richelieu*. Only a small audience attended on opening night, a situation the press blamed on a "suspicious" Boise public that had been "surfeited with trashy shows." Lindsay and his support found favor with the press which pointed out that although Luella Lindsay lacked "the requisite stage presence" as Parthenia, "her

action is almost faultless and her voice is splendidly adapted to the lines." The final evening Lindsay gave a "finished and powerful rendition of *Richelieu*" that the audience rewarded with "boisterous evidence of its approval." His "support was not what it should have been, being apparently unable to overcome the chill of a small house."[611]

Three events filled the last week of January. Anna Eyemann Bell gave a recital of an unspecified nature at the Sonna Opera House on the twenty-fifth.[612] Patrons packed the Columbia Theatre to the doors on January 27 to witness West's Big Minstrel Jubilee, a production featuring the nationally recognized talents of R. J. Jose and a supporting cast of equally skilled variety artists. Reviews described the novel "battleship Maine" setting of the show and labeled the acts as "high class except for one of two specialties."[613] *Boy Wanted* by the Charles E. Blaney Company made another Boise showing on January 27.[614]

Combined offerings at the Columbia Theatre and Sonna Opera House provided entertainments for almost every evening of the month in February of 1899 when over twenty performances filled the amusement calendar. A crowded auditorium at the Sonna Opera House on February 2 delighted at the "funmakers" in Fields and Clarks's company of colored entertainers.[615] Two days later the Kelly and Mason Company appeared in *Who Is Who?*.[616] Pinney booked the Ott Brothers' production of *All Aboard* with its "20 First Class Artists" into the Columbia for February 13 and 14. Mainly a vaudeville show, *All Aboard* had "few very clever productions and a great deal of unbridled horse play." A punning *Statesman* reviewer related that "good dancing and singing . . . relieved a condition that made those present feel they truly were 'all bored.'"[617] A local "Cake Walk and Colored Jubilee" at the Sonna Opera House on February 16 featured forty singers and twelve couples in the cakewalk competition for donated prizes.[618] On February 20 J. R. Wilson booked the Sonna Opera House for eleven evenings to show motion pictures of bull fights and other events with his $10,000 Edison projector.[619]

Also on February 20, the Jules Grau Opera Company returned for its second Boise appearance to begin a week's engagement at the Columbia Theatre. On opening night a packed house welcomed Grau's production of *Boccaccio* that earned press accolades for both the fine singing of Mary Carrington, Stanley Felch, George Broderick and Dan Young as well as the production's elaborate costuming. *The Mikado* on the next evening featured scenery illuminated by 200 incandescent lights and the singing of Fanny Myers and Harry Davis.[620] The remainder of the six performances by the Grau Company filled the Columbia each night. The presentation of *Falka* on February 24 included a "local hit" at the state legislature, then in session. The audience wildly applauded the following encore verse by Stanley Felch.

> "T'was down in Boise City,
> Where the legislators sit,
> I went up to the capital,
> To see how they did hit,
> T'was there I saw three ladies,
> Helping to make the law,
> I think they would look better
> In tights with Mr. Grau."[621]

At matinee and evening performances of *Olivette* and *The Brigands* on February 25, the Grau Opera Company completed a most rewarding season in Boise.[622]

The month concluded with a performance of *Faust* with Lewis Morrison on February 27 and the beginning of a week engagement by McEwen, the Scottish hypnotist on February 28. Morrison's production packed the Columbia Theatre where he was "accorded a royal ovation."[623] Miss Grace Maynard, "America's Most Wonderful Cataleptical Subject," and musician James McCoy assisted McEwen in his performance.[624]

Although performances declined in number during March, presentations of plays by Shakespeare and Sheridan lent a classical tone to the month. Sanford Dodge played the title role in his March 6 production of *Othello*. William Lloyd, in the role of Iago, played the role so poorly that half the members of an already small audience left before the end of the third act. The company performed well in the next evening's presentation of *The Prisoner of Spain*, a drama written by an unacknowledged actor in Dodge's troupe. However, only a "very abbreviated" audience showed up to appreciate the evening's efforts.[625] Classical music did little better than classical drama when the Max Bendix Company presented a recital of serious music on March 13. A trio, violin, soprano and piano, performing in the near freezing temperature of the Columbia, scored an artistic success, but did not attract much of an audience for its pains.[626] Three performances by the James-Kidder-Warde Company finally carried the day for classical drama. The company, under the management of Wagenhalls and Kemper, consisted of three nationally established stars—Louis James, Katherine Kidder and Frederick Warde—and a solid supporting cast of thirty-two. Even before the opening production of *The School for Scandal* on March 17, ticket sales were brisk with some dollar and a half tickets being scalped for five dollars. On the opening night of this major event in Boise theatre history, the audience packed the auditorium and forced Mr. Pinney to display the "Standing Room Only" sign early in the evening. Notices applauded Mr. James as Charles Surface, Mr. Warde as Joseph Surface and Miss Kidder as Lady Teazle and the excellent supporting actors including Mr. Landgon who performed "as good as the stars" in his role of Sir Peter Teazle. At the matinee next day James played the title role in *Hamlet* and that evening he appeared in *Macbeth* as

MacDuff with Warde as Macbeth and Miss Kidder as Lady Macbeth.[627]

April's entertainment offerings had little distinction to them except for the initial event, a return engagement at the Columbia by famed pianist Leopold Godowsky on the sixth.[628] Stuart Robinson in *The Meddler* on April 15 better fitted the public taste as the audience filled the auditorium to enjoy a "faultless" presentation in which the acting exceeded the merit of the play.[629] In a related item, the *Statesman* commented on how local theatre managers had been fooled by advance agents into booking shows of questionable or poor quality. In part the article read: "There was a time when Boise theatre-goers were surfeited and nauseated by outrageously rotten productions. Mr. Pinney has . . . 'gotten on' the barnstormers curves, and this season they have not had the opportunity of shifting scenery at the Columbia."[630]

On April 17 and 19 theatre patrons received a double dose of minstrelsy, one local amateur show by the Columbian Band at the Sonna Opera House and an appearance by the professionally prominent Primrose and Dockstader Company. Led by Professor Breach, the local minstrels filled the house for their performance.[631] Primrose and Dockstader's Minstrels also enjoyed a well-filled house at the Columbia, winning praise for the rich, beautiful settings, Dockstader's talents and the Carson's juggling act. The professional minstrels featured such "refined specialties" as the Deonzo trick barrel jumpers and champion high jumpers, a trio, the Quaker City Quartet and a "musical blacksmith."[632]

A presentation of *McSorley's Twins* with Bobby Gaylor began as scheduled on April 22 at the Columbia, but halted at the end of the first act when authorities attached the gate receipts as a result of some complicated contractual differences. With legal concerns straightened out Gaylor and company did a complete performance on April 24.[633] Nothing interfered with the showing of Charles Yale's

The Devil's Auction, a production often listed as *The Devil's Auction Forever*— due to the length of time it had been on tour before the American public. An extravaganza imitative of the historically significant and enormously popular *Black Crook*, Yale's show featured

Charles Yale's "The Devil's Auction"
University of Washington Libraries
Special Collections SG-D-2

elaborate scenery (including a "transformation" scene in which one full stage setting changed to another in full view of the audience), rousing Sousa marches, eight vaudeville acts plus a chorus made up of beautiful marching and dancing ladies dressed in tights. These mixed features, linked only together by a gossamer, thin plot, pleased the crowd at the Columbia on April 28.[634]

Six different groups presented a variety of plays and concerts during May. A popular priced traveling stock troupe, the Si Perkins Company, began a week's engagement on May 1 in *Uncle Dan'l* before a good but "chilly" audience. The press complained that the show suffered in comparison to a better rendition by the Bittner Company given in December. With such encouragement next night's production of *Aline, the Rose of Killarney* played to "a discouraging bunch of empty seats." Though attendance began to grow for the next few performances, the company left town on May 5 before completing its engagement, a condition that pleased audiences and probably came as a relief to Manager Pinney.[635] On May 8 the "Original Bostonians" appeared in an elaborate production of *Robin Hood*. Even at the advanced price of two and a half dollars for the best seats, the 850 people who filled the Columbia were "well repaid for attending" and shared a "memorable experience." Notices stressed the general and individual excellence of the acting and lauded sets and costumes.[636] Elmore Rice drew little more than a mention in the paper for his violin concert at the Methodist Church on May 10.[637] Blanche Walsh and Melbourne MacDonald attracted a great deal of attention for their acting in productions of *La Tosca* and *Fedora* on May 15 and 16 at the Columbia. As the review stated, "the curtain raised again and again" for the many curtain calls earned by the company.[638] In spite of the musical excellence displayed by the Bruno Steindel Company in their concert on May 20 at the Columbia, only a small audience attended. In an apologetic review a *Statesman* writer explained, "Boise is not musical, that is not in the classical sense. That has often been demonstrated, and last night furnished further evidence."[639] The "very fair house" that saw *McFadden's Row of Flats* on May 24 more aptly demonstrated the community taste in entertainment. Although the "exceedingly tiresome" comedians depended "entirely on twisted faces and heathenish attire to produce laughter," the audience did enjoy "clever dwarfs in a boxing specialty" and a trick bicycle rider plus "a genuine goat and an equally genuine pig."[640]

Following a rather well established summer pattern, the months of June, July and August had little to offer in the way of entertainments. Ten thousand people from Boise and the surrounding area crammed into the Ringling Brothers Circus tent on June 5.[641] Professor Bartholomew's Equine Extravaganza performed in a tent at 9th and Washington on July 3 and 4. Old time residents recognized the manager as George B. Bartholemew who had operated a small circus in Boise during the 1870's. His horse show, a good one, featured an equine "cakewalk."[642] The "Georgia Up-to Date Minstrels" paraded into town on July 28. These "30 colored stars" with their ten vaudeville novelties gave a poor performance. Redeemed only by a trombone solo, they gained only a fair-sized audience on opening night. The company refused to raise the curtain and had to refund ticket money when only thirteen people showed up for a planned second performance.[643] On August 31 Gentry's Famous Dog and Pony Show with its "250 Aristocratic Animal Actors" came to Boise to delight children and adults alike. Fifty cents admitted patrons to a tent erected on West 8th Street to see the well-trained animals, including the two smallest performing elephants in captivity.[644]

Regular theatrical events resumed on September 14 with the appearance of L. R. Stockwell in *The Midnight Bell*, a "picture of rural life" in which "comedy and pathos walked hand in hand."[645] The Bittner Theatre Company with its "well known favorites" returned once more to Boise on September 25 to play for a week at the Columbia Theatre during the Idaho Intermountain Fair. Some changes had been made in the troupe that now consisted of W. W. Bittner, William Smiley, Wallace Hooper, W.A. Clarke, J. B. Hymer, Mr. McClellan, Mr. Moran, E. H. Buchanan, Miss Mattie Choate, Miss Millie Stevens, Miss Jennie McAlpine, Mrs. Ella Bittner and Master Archie Buchanan. Bittner's company filled the Columbia for most of its shows before leaving on September 30. During the week Bittner presented *Drifting Apart, The Black Flag, A Deputy Sheriff, All a Mistake, Bulls and Bears* and *Jim the Penman*.[646]

October's eight amusements offered entertainment in a variety of forms. Hyde Gowan played classical music on his banjo in concert at the Sonna Opera House on October 2.[647] A week later the Metropolitan Opera Company presented *Mascot* and *The Bohemian Girl* at the Columbia Theatre under adverse conditions. Because the scenery and some costumes for the company's productions had been burned in the fire that destroyed the Auditorium Theatre in Pocatello during the company's previous engagement, the troupe opened in Boise without stage costumes and had to improvise settings from the Columbia Theatre's stock of house scenery. "Iceberg temperatures" in the auditorium added to the woes of the evening when the Columbia's heating system failed and a new furnace could not be installed before the performance. Negative press notices dealt a final blow to the opera troupe. The *Statesman* reviewer wrote that the audience, prepared for scenic shortcomings, hardly expected to hear "an opera with so few good voices." Singers found costumes to wear for the presentation of *The Bohemian Girl* the next evening, the performance went much better and, presumably, the heating improved, but only a small audience attended.[648] Fire had also affected the Thatcher Vaudeville and Vitascope Company that played the Sonna Opera House on October 12. While performing during the troupe's last engagement in Placerville, Idaho, a ceiling lamp fell and began a blaze that destroyed the performance hall and nearly consumed the town.

The remainder of October's entertainments managed to avoid calamities before arriving at the Columbia. Gus Hill's new version of *Vanity Fair*, "a mélange of the best of Burlesque and Vaudeville," entertained a large audience on October 19.[649] *Mistakes Will Happen* with the Charles Dickson Company, which followed on October 25, took a large audience "by storm" with its "unflawed" production and won favorable comparison to *Charley's Aunt* in a *Statesman* review that expressed gratitude that the show did not offer one of "these latter-day comedies usually so pregnant with cheap gallery ploys."[650] Evidently the management of Fritz and Webster's *A Breezy Time* displayed more cleverness in advertising than in the production of the farce comedy on October 28. Advertisements urged Boise theatre-goers to "C (see) the cat serenade, C the tennis quintette, C the three-legged sailor, etc." Notices found the production deserving of the small house it attracted and described it as having "a strong chestnutty appearance" with "short skirts, overly made-up comedians, stale jokes, and lots of cheap comedy."[651] With only the aid of rather formal advertising and the reputation of William Devere, noted character actor, *The Black Sheep* filled the Columbia to capacity on October 30.[652]

November's rather meager choice of entertainments included a minstrel show and a concert. Beach and Bowers' Minstrels, the "Monarchs of the Minstrel World," at the Columbia on the first of the month delighted a fair house even though the show "dragged in places" and, in the opinion of the press, was not "up to the standards of modern minstrelsy."[653] The following attraction, *My Friend from India* with Walter Jenkins and company, packed the house on the next evening with an audience which enjoyed the "roaring farce" even though a "high comedy" had been expected.[654] Even though the Boise public had experienced "a long string of one-nighters," a standing room only audience assembled at the Columbia on November 4 to see Arthur Donaldson star in *Yon Yonson*. Donaldson's fine comic acting and the music of the Lumberman's Quartet made hits with the crowd. Pretty scenery of a lumber camp in midwinter warranted press commentary, but the key mechanical effect, the breaking of a log jam, moved too slowly "to create the excitement the author intended." With new songs and specialties, the show stayed over for another night to offer the first Sunday night attraction in the history of Boise. James Pinney used the performance as a test to see if the Boise public would support Sunday shows. Although only 250 people attended the performance on Sunday, the paper reported Manager Pinney as pleased with the experiment.[655] Weeks passed before the next diversion. The Schubert Symphony Club played in concert at the Columbia on November 27 before a fair audience that accorded the artists' program many encores.[656] Even though the press described the performance of *The Romance of Coon Hollow* on November 30 as "far from satisfactory," the show attracted a large crowd eager to see such publicized features as "the torpedo sensation, the steamboat race [and] the cotton press tragedy."[657]

December began with two combination shows and ended with a stock theatre season. The numerous vaudeville specialties in the Hoyt Company's production of *A Stranger in New York* entertained a large house on December 5 at the Columbia Theatre.[658] The next evening Edwin Mayo, in a stage version of Mark Twain's *Puddin'head Wilson*, delighted another large audience. Notices praised the play as "one of the best" and hailed its star as a "worthy son of Frank Mayo," a popular star in melodramas during the 1870's.[659] The year's amusements ended with a week of plays by the Noble Dramatic Company during the Christmas

George Noble
University of Washington
Libraries Special Collections
UW13257

season. The troupe opened at the Columbia on Christmas Day with *Our Strategists* and ended the engagement on December 30, with matinee and evening shows of *The Gold King* and *Fanchon the Cricket*. During the season Noble also presented *Reuben Glue*, *East Lynne* and *The Train Wreckers*. For the most part the company enjoyed good patronage with fair sized to full houses for all performances.[660]

These performances by the Noble Dramatic Company marked the end of Boise theatre entertainments in the nineteenth century, a century that had witnessed the growth of the city and the number of performances for its citizens. After an impressive beginning in the gold camps of the Boise Basin and the first shows in Boise's Idaho Saloon, theatre barely endured during lean years of the 1870's. A railroad route to the city established in 1883 opened the community to national touring organizations. Even then Boise lacked a modern performance facility until the Columbia Theatre was erected in 1892 to host the road shows and touring repertory players. It would still be some years before Boise would be recognized as a "show town," a community that embraced a variety of theatrical entertainments and by its attendance provide adequate economic

compensation to attract road shows and traveling repertory companies of professional quality.

In the last decade of the nineteenth century Boise attracted barely an average of one hundred entertainments a year. In the early years of the twentieth century the vital rail connection, a well appointed theatre venue and a citizenry eager for amusement would spur a three and four fold growth in entertainments. Boise, Idaho was at last truly a "show town."

CHAPTER 4 NOTES

[381] *Idaho Daily Statesman*, May 8, 1890, p. 2; May 13, 1890, p. 3.

[382] *Ibid.*, September 27, 1890, p. 4.

[383] *Ibid.*, October 25, 1890, p. 4.

[384] *Ibid.*, January 5, 1890, p. 3; January 7, 1890, p. 3; January 8, 1890, p. 3.

[385] *Ibid.*, March 1, 1890, p. 3; March 8, 1890, p. 3; March 11, 1890, p. 3.

[386] *Ibid.*, March 11, 1890, p. 3.

[387] *Ibid.*, March 12, 1890, p. 3.

[388] *Ibid.*

[389] *Ibid.*, May 16, 1890, p. 3.

[390] *Ibid.*, August 24, 1890, p. 4;

[391] *Ibid.*, October 15, 1890, p. 4; October 22, 1890, p. 2; October 28, 1890, p. 4.

[392] *Ibid.*, November 1, 1890, pp. 3, 4; November 4, 18890, p. 4; November 5, 1890, pp. 3 , 4; November 6, 1890, pp. 3, 4; November 7, 1890, pp. 3,4; November 8, 1890, p. 3; November 9, 1890, p. 4.

[393] *Ibid.*, May 9, 1890, p. 2.

[394] *Ibid.*, July 10, 1890, p. 3.

[395] *Ibid.*, September 14, 1890, p. 4.

[396] *Ibid.*, June 18, 1890, p. 3.

[397] *Ibid.*, August 2, 1890, p. 4.

[398] *Ibid.*, November 11, 1890, p. 4; November 13, 1890, p. 4; November 14, 1890, p. 4; November 19, 1890, p. 4.

[399] *Ibid.*, December 28, 1890, p. 8.

[400] *Ibid.*, January 21, 1891, p. 5; January 22, 1891, p. 8.

[401] *Ibid.*, February 15, 1891, p. 6.

[402] *Ibid.*, February 17, 1891, p. 8; February 18, 1891, p. 8; February 19, 1891, p. 8; February 20, 181, p. 8.

[403] *Ibid.*, December 15, 1891, p. 8; December 16, 1891, p. 8; December 17, 1891, p. 8.

[404] *Ibid.*, March 24, 1891, p. 8.

[405] *Ibid.*, April 5, 1891, p. 8.

[406] *Ibid.*, April 12, 1891, p. 8; April 14,1891, p. 8; April 15, 1891, p. 8.

[407] *Ibid.*, May 7, 1891, p. 5.

[408] *Ibid.*, June 13, 1891, p. 8; June 14, 1891, p. 8; June 16, 1891, p. 8; June 18, 1891, p. 8; June 26, 1891, p. 8.

[409] *Ibid.*, September 11, 1891, p. 3.

410   *Ibid.*, September 20, 1891, p. 6; September 22, 1891 p. 8; September 23, 1891, p. 8; September 24. 18991, p. 8;September 26, 1891, p. 8; September 27, 1891, p. 8.

411   *Ibid.*, October 7, 1891, p. 3; October 25. 1891, p. 8; October 27, 1891, p. 8.

412   *Ibid.*, December 13, 1891, p. 7.

413   *Ibid.*, December 15, 1891, p. 3; December 22, 1891, p. 5; December 23, 1891, p. 5; December 24, 1891, p. 8; December 25, 1891, p. 8; December 26, 1891, p. 8; December 29, 1891, p. 8; December 31, 1891, p. 5.

414   *Ibid.*, April 8, 1892, p. 8; April 13, 1892, p. 5; April 19, 1892, p. 8; April 20, 1892, p. 8.

415   *Ibid.*, January 5, 1892, p. 5.

416   *Ibid.*, February 21, 1892, p. 1; February 23, 1892, p. 8; February 24, 1892, p. 8; February 25, 1892, p. 8; February 26, 1892, p. 8.

417   *Ibid.*, March 11, 1892, p. 5; April 9, 1892, p. 6.

418   *Ibid.*, April 27, 1892, p. 4; April 30, 1892, p. 5.

419   *Ibid.*, May 1, 1892, p. 2.

420   *Ibid.*, May 19, 1892, p. 5.

421   *Ibid.*, May 17, 1892, p. 4; May, 19, 1892, p. 8.

422   *Ibid.*, May 25, 1892, p. 6.

423   *Ibid.*, June 4, 1892, p. 2.

424   *Ibid.*, June 26, 1892, p. 2; June 30, 1892, p. 8.

425   *Ibid.*, August 24, 1892, p. 2; October 21, 1892, p. 5; November 6, 1892, p. 3.

426   *Ibid.*, April 26, 1892, p. 1; July 14, 1892, p. 4; July 15, 1892, p. 5; September 6, 1892, p. 5.

427   *Ibid.*, November 20, 1892, p. 3.

428   *Ibid.*, November 23, 1892, p. 5; December 6, 1892, p. 8; December 12, 1892, p. 4; December 13, 1892, p. 1.

429   *Ibid.*, May 29, 1892, p. 8; December 12, 1892, p. 4.

430   *Ibid.*, April 30, 1892, p. 8; June 1, 1892, p. 8.

431   *Ibid.*, July 23, 1892, p. 8.

432   *Ibid.*, December 6, 1892, p. 8.

433   *Ibid.*, December 12, 1892, p. 4.

434   *Ibid.*, December 13, 1892, p. 1.

435   *Ibid.*, January 28, 1893, p. 5.

436   *Ibid.*, May 12, 1893, p. 8; May 17, 1893, p. 8; My 20, 1893, p. 5; June 25, 1893, p. 8; July 5, 1893, p. 8; September 29, 1893, p. 8; December 14, 1893, p. 6.

437 *Ibid.*, January 5, 1893, p. 8.
438 *Ibid.*, January 10 1893, p. 4.
439 *Ibid.*, January 13, 1893, ; p. 1.
440 *Ibid.*, January 13, 1893, p. 5; January 18, 1893, p. 8; January 19, 1893, p. 8; January 20, 1893, p. 5; January 21, 1893, p. 5.
441 *Ibid.*, February 26, 1893, p. 8.
442 *Ibid.*, February 24, 1893, p. 3; February 26, 1893, p. 8; February 28, 1893, p. 8.
443 *Ibid.*, March 25, 1893, p. 2; March 31, 1893, p. 8.
444 *Ibid.*, April 26, 1893, p. 3.
445 *Ibid.*, April 28, 1893, p. 3; May 3, 1893, p. 3; May 4, 1893, p. 8; May 6, 1893, p. 5.
446 *Ibid.*, July 13, 1893, p. 2; July 15, 1893, p. 5.
447 *Ibid.*, July 13, 1893, p. 6.
448 *Ibid.*, September 5, 1893, p. 6.
449 Phyllis Hartnoll, ed., *The Oxford Companion To The Theatre*, 2nd ed. (London: Oxford University Press, 1957), p. 199.
450 *Idaho Daily Statesman*, October 14, 1893, p. 6.
451 *Ibid.*, October 17, 1893, p. 6.
452 *Ibid.*, October 31, 1893, p. 3.
453 *Ibid.*, November 2, 1893, p. 3; November 24, 1893, p. 6; November 25, 1893, p. 3.
454 *Ibid.*, December 24, 1893, pp. 5, 6; December 28, 1893, p. 3; December 29, 1893, p. 6.
455 *Ibid.*, February 1, 1893, p. 8; February 15, 1893, p. 5; February 22, 1893, p. 2; February 24, 1893, p. 8.
456 *Ibid.*, May 2, 1893, p. 8.
457 *Ibid.*, December 3, 1893, p. 1.
458 *Ibid.*, May 12, 1893, p. 3; May 26, 1893, p. 3.
459 *Ibid.*, June 13, 1893, p. 8.
460 *Ibid.*, December 15, 1893, p. 6.
461 *Ibid.*, January 2, 1894, p. 3; January 14, 1894, p. 3.
462 *Ibid.*, February 25, 1894, p. 3; February 28, 1894, p. 6.
463 *Ibid.*, April 10, 1894, p. 6.
464 *Ibid.*, April 20, 1894, p. 3.
465 *Ibid.*, May 16, 1894, p. 2.
466 *Ibid.*, May 16, 1894, p. 4; May 22, 1894, p. 1.
467 *Ibid.*, May 30, 1894, p. 2; June 3, 1894, p. 3.
468 *Ibid.*, June 2, 1894, p. 2; June 13, 1894, p. 3.
469 *Ibid.*, June 19, 1894, p. 3.

470   *Ibid.*, June 30, 1894, p. 2.

471   *Ibid.*, July 10, 1894, p. 6; July 12, 1894, p. 3.

472   *Ibid.*, August 11, 1894, p. 3; August 16, 1894, p. 6.

473   *Ibid.*, August 28, 1894, p. 6; August 29, 1894, p. 6.

474   *Ibid.*, September 16, 1894, p. 3; September 19, 1894, p. 6.

475   *Ibid.*, September 29, 1894, pp. 4, 6; October 2, 1894, p. 6.

476   *Ibid.*, October 1, 1894, p. 4.

477   *Ibid.*, September 30, 1894, p. 6.

478   *Ibid.*, October 14, 1894, p. 3; October 21, 1894, p. 6.

479   *Ibid.*, October 24, 1894, p. 4; October 30, 1894, p. 6.

480   *Ibid.*, November 3, 1894, p. 4.

481   *Ibid.*, November 17, 1894, p. 6; November 20, 1894, p. 4; November 24, 1894, p. 3.

482   *Ibid.*, November 29, 1894, p. 4; November 30, 1894, p. 6.

483   *Ibid.*, December 6, 1894, p. 4; December 7, 1894, p. 3.

484   *Ibid.*, December 11, 1894, p. 3.

485   *Ibid.*, December 31, 1894, p.3.

486   *Ibid.*, January 1, 1895, p. 6; January 2, 1895, p. 1; January 3, 1895, p. 6.

487   *Ibid.*, January 10, 1895, p. 6; January 14, 1895, p. 6; January 19, 1895, p. 6; January 23, 1895, p. 6.

488   *Ibid.*, January 20, 1895, p. 4; January 27, p. 6.

489   *Ibid.*, January 29, 1895, p. 6.

490   *Ibid.*, January 29, 1895, p. 4; February 1, 1895, p. 6; February 2, 1895, p. 4; February 3, 1895, p. 6.

491   *Ibid.*, February 8, 1895, p. 3; February 15, 1895, p. 3; February 17, 1895, p. 6.

492   *Ibid.*, February 12, 1895, pp. 3, 6; February 15, 1895, p. 6; February 17, 1895, p. 6; February 19, 1895, p. 3; February 20, 1895, p. 6; February 21, 1895, p. 3; February 22, 1895, p. 3.

493   *Ibid.*, February 20, 1895, p. 4; February 22, 1895, p. 3; February 23, 1895, p. 6.

494   *Ibid.*, March 14, 1895, p. 6; March 16, 1895, p. 3; March 19, 1895, p. 3; March 22, 1895, p. 3.

495   *Ibid.*, March 20, 1895, p. 3; March 24, 1895, p. 5; April 9, 1895, p. 4; April 18, 1895, p. 3; April 19, 1895, p. 6; April 20, 1895, p. 4; April 21, 1895, p. 6; April 25, 1895, p. 3.

496   *Ibid.*, May 7, 1895, p. 3; May 8, 1895, p. 6; May 9, 1895, p. 6.

497   *Ibid.*, May 15, 1895, p. 6.

498   *Ibid.*, May 12, 1895, p. 3; May 18, 1895, p. 3; May 19, 1895, p. 6.

499 *Ibid.*, May 24, 1895, p. 4; May 28, 1895, p. 3; May 29, 1895, p. 6; June 4, 1895, p. 6; June 7, 1895, p. 6.

500 *Ibid.*, May 30, 1895, p. 3; June 2, 1895, p. 3.

501 *Ibid.*, June 4, 1895, p. 4; June 11, 1895, p. 6.

502 *Ibid.*, June 13, 1895, p. 3; June 14, 1895, p. 3; June 15, 1895, p. 3.

503 *Ibid.*, July 2, 1895, p. 6; July 21, 1895, p. 6; July 27, 1895, p. 6.

504 *Ibid.*, August 3, 1895, p. 4; August 10, 1895, p. 6.

505 *Ibid.*, September 8, 1895, p. 3.

506 *Ibid.*, September 18, 1895, p. 5; September 19, 1895, p. 6; September 21, 1895, p. 6; September 24, 1895, p. 3; September 25, 1895, pp. 4, 6; September 26, 1895, pp. 4, 6; September 27, 1895, p. 4; September 28, 1895, p. 3; September 29, 1895, p. 6.

507 *Ibid.*, October 1, 1895, p. 6; October 3, 1895, p. 3; October 11, 1895, p. 3.

508 *Ibid.*, October 9, 1895, p. 3; October 13, 1895, p. 3; October 26, 1895, p. 3; November 1, 1895, p. 6.

509 *Ibid.*, November 3, 1895, p. 3; November 9, 1895, p. 3.

510 *Ibid.*, November 9, 1895, p. 3; November 12, 1895, p. 6; November 13, 1895, p. 6.

511 *Ibid.*, November 7, 1895, p. 4; November 14, 1895, p. 3.

512 *Ibid.*, November 12, 1895, p. 3; November 15, 1895, p. 3.

513 *Ibid.*, November 26, 1895, p. 3; November 29, 1895, p. 6.

514 *Ibid.*, November 30, 1895, p. 4; December 4, 1895, p. 6; December 10, 1895, p. 6.

515 *Ibid.*, November 29, 1895, p. 4; December 4, 1895, p. 1.

516 *Ibid.*, December 4, 1895, p. 3; December 6, 1895, p. 3.

517 *Ibid.*, December 7, 1895, p. 6; December 10, 1895, p. 2; December 13, 1895, p. 6.

518 *Ibid.*, December 12, 1895, p. 3.

519 *Ibid.*, January 5, 1896, p. 6; January 7, 1896, p. 3; January 8, 1896, p. 3; January 9, 1896, p. 3; January 10, 1896, p. 6; January 11, 1896, p. 6; January 12, 1896, p. 8.

520 *Ibid.*, January 12, 1896, p. 8; January 15, 1896, p. 6; January 16, 1896, p. 3.

521 *Ibid.*, January 14, 1896, p. 6; January 18, 1896, p. 3.

522 *Ibid.*, January 29, 1896, p. 6.

523 *Ibid.*, January 30, 1896, p. 3; January 31, 1896, p. 3.

524 *Ibid.*, February 1, 1896, p. 3; February 2, 1896, p. 5.

525   *Ibid.*, February 4, 1896, p. 3; February 6, 1896, p. 6; February 7, 1896, p. 6.

526   *Ibid.*, February 25, 1896, p. 6; February 26, 1896, p. 6.

527   *Ibid.*, March 10, 1896, p. 3; March 17, 1896, p. 3; March 18, 1896, p. 6.

528   *Ibid.*, March 19, 1896, p. 4; March 24, 1896, p. 3; March 25, 1896, p. 3

529   *Ibid.*, April 10, 1896, p. 3; April 11, 1896, p. 6; April 14, 1896, p. 3; April 17, 1896, p. 6.

530   *Ibid.*, May 9, 1896, p. 3; May 13, 1896, p. 3; May 14, 1896, p. 3; May 15, 1896, p. 6.

531   *Ibid.*, May 16, 1896, p. 3; May 19, 1896, p. 3.

532   *Ibid.*, June 14, 1896, p. 6; June 23, 1896, p. 3.

533   *Ibid.*, September 2, 1896, p. 3; September 3, 1896, p. 3; September 18, 1896, p. 6; September 20, 1896, p. 3; September 22, 1896, p. 3; September 23, 1896, p. 3; September 25, 1896, p. 6; September 27, 1896, p. 3; September 29, 1896, p. 3.

534   *Ibid.*, October 2, 1896, p. 6; October 4, 1896, p. 3.

535   *Ibid.*, October 3, 1896, p. 6; October 6, 1896, p. 6

536   *Ibid.*, October 18, 1896, p. 7; October 20, 1896, p. 3.

537   *Ibid.*, December 7, 1896, p. 2; December 9, 1896, p. 3.

538   *Ibid.*, January 2, 1897, p. 4.

539   *Ibid.*, January 10, 1897, p. 6; January 12, 1897, p. 6.

540   *Ibid.*, January 23, 1897, p. 3; January 24. 1897, p. 6.

541   *Ibid.*, February 19, 1897, p. 4; February 25, 1897, p. 3.

542   *Ibid.*, March 3, 1897, p. 6; March 4, 1897, p. 6.

543   *Ibid.*, March 5, 1897, p. 2; March 5, 1897, p. 6; March 6, 1897, p. 6.

544   *Ibid.*, March 14, 1897, p. 3.

545   *Ibid.*, March 27, 1897, p. 6; March 28, 1897, p. 2.

546   *Ibid.*, March 30, 1897, p. 6.

547   *Ibid.*, April 6, 1897, p. 4; April 10, 1897, p. 6; April 14, 1897, p. 6; April 13, 1897, p. 3; April 17, 1897, p. 6.

548   *Ibid.*, April 21, 1897.

549   *Ibid.*, April 16, 197, p. 3; April 19, 1897, p. 6; April 20, 1897, p. 6; April 21, 1897, p. 6; April 23, 1897, p. 3; April 25, 1897, p. 6; April 27, 1897, pp. 3, 6; April 28, 1897, p. 6; April 29, 1897, p. 3; April 30, 1897, p. 6; May, 1, 1897, p. 3.

550   *Ibid.*, May 4, 1897, p. 6; May 5, 1897, p. 3.

551   *Ibid.*, May 1, 1897, p. 3; May 6, 1897, p. 3; May 7, 1897, p. 3.

552   *Ibid.*, May 11, 1897, p. 3; May 15, 1897, p. 3.

553   *Ibid.*, June 8, 1897, p. 6.

554   *Ibid.*, July 26, 1897, p. 6; July 28, 1897, p. 3; July 30, 1897, p. 3; July 31, 1897, p. 6.

555   *Ibid.*, September 16, 1897, p. 6; September 17, 1897, p. 3; September 18, 1897, p. 3.

556   *Ibid.*, September 28, 1897, pp. 3, 4; September 29, 1897, p. 3.

557   *Ibid.*, October 5, 1897, p. 3.

558   *Ibid.*, October 20, 1897, p. 3; October 23, 1897, pp. 4.

559   *Ibid.*, October 25, 1897, p. 4; October 26, 1897, p. 6; October 31, 1897, p. 3.

560   *Ibid.*, November 2, 1897, p. 6; November 3, 1897, p. 4; November 4, 1897, p. 6.

561   *Ibid.*, November 3, 1897, p. 6; November 9, 1897, p. 3; November 10, 1897, p. 3.

562   *Ibid.*, November 15, 1897, p. 6; November 18, 1897, p. 6; November 20, 1897, p. 6; November 21, 1897, p. 4.

563   *Ibid.*, November 21, 1897, p. 5; November 27, 1897, p. 6.

564   *Ibid.*, December 16, 1897, p. 3; December 21, 1897, p. 3

565   *Ibid.*, December 18, 1897, p. 4; December 23, 1897, p. 3.

566   *Ibid.*, December 19, 1897, p. 4.

567   *Ibid.*, December 26, 1897, p. 6.

568   *Ibid.*, December 25, 1897, p. 4; December 30, 1897, p. 6.

569   *Ibid.*, December 26, 1897, p. 6.

570   *Ibid.*, January 1, 1898, p. 3; January 7, 1898, p. 6; January 8, 1898, p. 6; January 9, 1898, p. 8.

571   *Ibid.*, January 20, 1898, p. 2; January 27, 1898, p. 3.

572   *Ibid.*, January 31, 1898, p. 4; February 2, 1898, p. 2; February 4, 1898, p. 6; February 8, 1898, p. 6.

573   *Ibid.*, February 9, 1898, p. 6.

574   *Ibid.*, February 10, 1898, p. 3; February 11, 1898, p. 6; February 12, 1898, p. 6; February 13, 1898, p. 3.

575   *Ibid.*, February 26, 1898, p. 6; March 1, 1898, p. 6; March 5, 1898, p. 3.

576   *Ibid.*, March 6, 1898, p. 6; March 8, 1898, p. 6; March 9, 1898, p. 6; March 10, 1898, p. 6; March 11, 1898, p. 6; March 12, 1896, p. 3; March 13, 1898, p. 7; March 15, 1898, p. 6; March 16, 1898, p. 6; March 17, 1898, p. 3; March 18, 1898, p. 6; March 19, 1898, p. 3.

577   *Ibid.*, March 10, 1898, p. 6; March 15, 1898, p. 6.

578   *Ibid.*, March 16, 1898, p. 3; March 17, 1898, p. 3; March 18, 1898, p. 6; March 19, 1898, p. 3; March 20, 1898, p. 2; March 22, 1898, p. 6; March 23, 1898, p. 3; March 24, 1898, p. 6; March 25, 1898, p. 6; March 26, 1898, p. 6; March 27, 1898, p. 2; March 29, 1898, p. 6; March 30, 1898, p. 6.

579   *Ibid.*, April 3, 1898, p. 6; April 9, 1898, p. 6; April10, 1898, p. 6.

580   *Ibid.*, April 11, 1898, p. 4; April 14, 1898, p. 6.

581   *Ibid.*, April 14, 1898, p. 4; April 15, 1898, p. 6.

582   *Ibid.*, April 21, 1898, p. 6; April 22, 1898, ;. 6.

583   *Ibid.*, April 28, 1898, p. 6; April 29, 1898, p. 6.

584   *Ibid.*, May 4, 1898, p. 6; May 5, 1898, p. 6.

585   *Ibid.*, April 29, 1898, p. 6.

586   *Ibid.*, May 2, 1898, p. 4; May 3, 1898, p. 3; May 7, 1898, p. 6.

587   *Ibid.*, May 1, 1898, p. 4; May 8, 1898, p. 4.

588   *Ibid.*, May 13, 1898, p. 4; May 17, 1898, p. 6; May 18, 1898, p. 6; May 19, 1898, p. 6; May 21, 1898, p. 3.

589   *Ibid.*, June 9, 1898, p. 6; June 9, 1898, p. 6.

590   *Ibid.*, June 11, 1898, p. 6.

591   *Ibid.*, June 26, 1898, p. 6; June 30, 1898, p. 6; July 2, 1898, p. 6.

592   *Ibid.*, August 3, 1898, p. 6.

593   *Ibid.*, September 30, 1898, p. 5; October 3, 1898, p. 4.

594   *Ibid.*, October 2, 1898, p. 4.

595   *Ibid.*, October 4, 1898, p. 5; October 5, 1898, pp. 4, 5; October 6, 1898, p. 5; October 7, 1898, p. 5; October 8, 1898, pp. 4, 5.

596   *Ibid.*, October 18, 1898, p. 6.

597   *Ibid.*, October 17, 1898, p. 4; October 25, 1898, p. 4; October 28, 1898, p. 6

598   *Ibid.*, October 29, 1898, p. 6; November 4, 1898, p. 6.

599   *Ibid.*, November 10, 1898, p. 6.

600   *Ibid.*, November 20, 1898, p. 4.

601   *Ibid.*, November 25, 1898, p. 6; December 2, 1898, p. 6.

602   *Ibid.*, December 2, 1898, p. 6; December 9, 1898, p. 3.

603   *Ibid.*, December 5, 1898, p. 4; December 9, 1898, p. 3; December 11, 1898, p. 4.

604   *Ibid.*, December 11, 1898, pp. 3, 4; December 16, 1898, p. 6

605   *Ibid.*, December 11, 1898, p. 3; December 17, 1898, p. 4.

606   *Ibid.*, December 22, 1898, p. 4; December 24, 1898, p. 5; December 28, 1898, p. 6; December 29, 1898, p. 6; December 30, 1898, p. 6; December 31, 1898, p. 6.

607   *Ibid.*, January 1, 1899, p. 6; January 5, 1899, p. 6.

608   *Ibid.*, January 3, 1899, p. 6; January 5, 1899, p. 6; January 9, 1899, p. 6.

609   *Ibid.*, January 7, 1889, p. 4; January 11, 1899, p. 6.

610   *Ibid.*, January 17, 1899, p. 4; January 21, 1899, p. 6.

611   *Ibid.*, January 22, 1899, p. 2; January 24, 1899, p. 3; January 25, 1899, p. 4.

612   *Ibid.*, January 23, 1899, p. 2.

613   *Ibid.*, January 22, 1899, p. 2; January 28, 1899, p. 3.

614   *Ibid.*, January 28, 1899, p. 6.

615   *Ibid.*, January 31, 1899, p. 4; February 2, 1899, p. 6; February 3, 1899, p. 6.

616   *Ibid.*, February 3, 1899, p. 6.

617   *Ibid.*, February 7, 1899, p. 4; February 14, 1899, p. 4.

618   *Ibid.*, February 16, 1899, p. 4.

619   *Ibid.*, February 21, 1899, pp. 3, 6.

620   *Ibid.*, February 21, 1899, p. 3.

621   *Ibid.*, February 25, 1899, p. 6.

622   *Ibid.*, February 25, 1899, p. 6; February 26, 1899, p. 5.

623   *Ibid.*, February 28, 1899, p. 6.

624   *Ibid.*, February 23, 1899, p. 4.

625   *Ibid.*, March 3, 1899, p. 4; March 7, 1899, p. 4; March 8, 1899, p. 6.

626   *Ibid.*, March 8, 1899, p. 6; March 14, 1899, p. 4.

627   *Ibid.*, March 12, 1899, p. 4; March 11, 1899, p. 4; March 17, 1899, p. 4; March 18, 1899, p. 4; March 19, 1899, p. 5;

628   *Ibid.*, April 1, 1899, p. 6.

629   *Ibid.*, April 7, 1899, p. 6; April 16, 1899, p. 6.

630   *Ibid.*, April 16, 1899, p. 6.

631   *Ibid.*, April 11, 1899, p. 6; April 18, 1899, p. 3.

632   *Ibid.*, April 14, 1899, p. 6; April 20, 1899, p. 8.

633   *Ibid.*, April 23, 1899, p. 4; April 24, 1899, p. 4.

634   *Ibid.*, April 28, 1899, p. 3; April 29, 1899, p. 6.

635   *Ibid.*, April 30, 1899, p. 4; May 2, 1899, p. 4; May 3, 1899, p. 3; May 4, 1899, p. 5; May 5. 1899, p. 6; May 6, 1899, p. 6.

636   *Ibid.*, April 30, 1899, p. 4; May 9, 1899, p. 6.

637   *Ibid.*, May 10, 1899, p. 6.

638   *Ibid.*, May 10, 1899, p. 4; May 16, 1899, p. 6

639   *Ibid.*, May 19, 1899, p. 4; May 21, 1899, p. 6.

640   *Ibid.*, May 25, 1899, p. 8.

641   *Ibid.*, June 5, 1899, p. 3-

642   *Ibid.*, July 2, 1899, p. 8; July 4, 1899, p. 6

643   *Ibid.*, July 27, 1899, p. 4; July 29, 1899, p. 6; July 30, 1899, p. 6.

644   *Ibid.*, August 31, 1899, p. 4.

645   *Ibid.*, September 14, 1899, p. 2; September 15, 1899, p. 6.

646   *Ibid.*, September 23, 1899, p. 3; September 26, 1899, pp. 2, 6; September 27, 1899, p. 2; September 28, 1899, p. 2; September 29, 1899, p. 2; September 30, 1899, p. 6.

647   *Ibid.*, September 29, 1899, p. 6.

648   *Ibid.*, October 4, 1899, p. 4; October 10, 1899, p. 4; October 11, 1899, p. 6.

649   *Ibid.*, October 13, 1899, p. 4; October 18, 1899, p. 6, October 20, 1899, p. 6.

650   *Ibid.*, October 20, 1899, p. 4; October 26, 1899, p. 6.

651   *Ibid.*, October 25, 1899, pp. 4, 5; October 29, 1899, p. 6.

652   *Ibid.*, October 29, 1899, p.4; October 31, 1899, p. 6.

653   *Ibid.*, October 29, 1899, p. 6; November 2, 1899, p. 3.

654   *Ibid.*, October 29, 1899, p. 6; November 3, 1899, p. 6.

655   *Ibid.*, October 31, 1899, p. 3; November 5, 1899, p. 5; November 7, 1899, p. 6.

656   *Ibid.*, November 24, 1899, p. 4; November 28, 1899, p. 4.

657   *Ibid.*, November 25, 1899, pp. 4 , 6; December 1, 1899, p. 8.

658   *Ibid.*, December 6, 1899, p. 6.

659   *Ibid.*, December 6, 1899, p. 4; December 7, 1899, p. 4.

660   *Ibid.*, December 19, 1899, p. 6; December 22, 1899, p. 6; December 26, 1899, p. 4; December 27, 1899, pp. 4, 6; December 28, 1899, p. 4; December 29, 1899, p. 4; December 30, 1899, p. 6.

Bibliography

Bird, Anna Laurie. *Boise: The Peace Valley*. Caldwell, Idaho: The Caxston Printer, Ltd., 1934.

Boise News (Idaho City, Idaho)

Ernst, Alice Henson. *Trouping the Oregon Country*. Portland, Oregon: Oregon Historical Society, 1961.

Gilliard, Fred. "Early Theatre in the Owyhees," *Idaho Yesterdays*. Summer, 1973.

Hart, Arthur A. *Basin of Gold: Life in the Boise Basin: 1862-1890*. Boise, Idaho: Lithocraft, Inc., 1986.

Hartnoll, Phylliss. *The Oxford Companion to the Theatre*, 2nd Edition. London: Oxford University Press, 1957.

Idaho Daily Statesman (Boise, Idaho)

Idaho Tri-Weekly Statesman (Boise, Idaho)

Idaho World (Idaho City, Idaho)

Lauterbach, Charles. "Theatre in Idaho City: 1863-1864," *Idaho Magazine*. March, 2007. Vol. 6, No. 6.

Lauterbach, Charles. "Theatre in Idaho City: 1865-1866," *Idaho Magazine*. April, 2007. Vol. 6, No. 7.

MacGregor, Carol. *Boise, Idaho, 1882-1910: Prosperity in Isolation.* Missoula, Montana: Mountain Press Publishing Co., 2006

Morris, Lloyd. *Curtain Time.* New York: Random House, 1953.

New York Mirror

Owyhee Avalanche (Silver City, Idaho)

Schoberlin, Melvin. *From Candles to Footlights.* Denver: Old West Publishing Co., 1941.

Schwarz, Lyle. "Theatre on the Gold Frontier: A Cultural Study of Five Northwest Towns." Ph.D diss., Washington State University, 1975.

Smith, Sol. *Theatrical Management.* New York: Benjamin Blom, Inc., 1968. Reprint of 1868 edition.

Watson, Margaret G. *Silver Theatre: Amusements of Nevada's Mining Frontier, 1850-1864.* Glendale, California: Arthur H. Clark Co., 1964.

Wells, Merle. *Boise: An Illustrated History.* Woodland, California: Winston Publications, Inc., 1982.

Index

www.ingramcontent.com/pod-product-compliance
Lightning Source LLC
Chambersburg PA
CBHW022127080426
42734CB00006B/255